The Complete Guide to Hoodoo Magic

by Powerful Rootwork Spells for Protection, Love, Luck, and Financial Success

The Complete Guide to Hoodoo Magic

First Edition: 2026

TABLE OF CONTENTS

INTRODUCTION

For countless generations, the true essence of Hoodoo has been obscured by misconceptions, often dismissed as mere superstition or relegated to the shadows of history. Yet, for those who truly listen, the earth itself whispers its ancient secrets, revealing a profound and practical magic that is as alive today as it was centuries ago. This isn't a complex, inaccessible form of magic reserved for a select few; it is a vibrant, living current, a direct spiritual inheritance, woven into the fabric of everyday life, waiting for you to reclaim its power. It speaks through the rustle of leaves, the scent of a brewing herb, the glint of an old coin, offering tangible pathways to reshape your reality. You don't need elaborate tools or hidden knowledge to begin; you already possess the most potent instrument of all: your intention, guided by the wisdom of those who walked before us, waiting to be awakened.

Perhaps you've felt it—a lingering sense of unease, an invisible weight pressing down, or a frustrating stagnation that blocks your path to joy and success. You've yearned for a way to safeguard your space, to clear the heavy energies that drain your spirit, or to attract the blessings of prosperity and love you rightfully deserve. The world can feel chaotic, unpredictable, and sometimes, actively hostile, leaving you feeling adrift, vulnerable, or powerless against unseen forces or persistent setbacks. You crave more than fleeting self-help platitudes; you seek concrete actions, reliable rituals, and a clear understanding of how to reclaim your agency and create tangible, positive change in your life. It's a natural human desire to protect what is sacred, to manifest abundance, and to walk through life with an unwavering sense of inner strength, yet finding a genuine, effective, and respectful path to achieve this can feel like searching for a hidden spring in a vast desert. You're ready to move beyond simply wishing for a better reality; you're ready to learn *exactly what to do* to bring that reality into being.

Imagine waking each day feeling enveloped in a profound sense of spiritual protection, knowing that your home is a sanctuary and your energy is shielded from negativity. Picture yourself confidently navigating life's challenges, armed with practical techniques to clear obstacles and attract genuine opportunities. Envision a life where you understand the subtle language of intention, where simple, everyday actions become powerful conduits for manifesting prosperity, love, and success. This isn't a fantastical dream; it is the concrete, achievable transformation that awaits you within the pages of this guide. You will move from feeling overwhelmed and stuck to embodying a powerful, intentional presence, grounded in ancient wisdom and equipped with practical skills. The shift will be palpable, a quiet revolution in your daily existence, transforming your worries into clarity and your hopes into tangible realities, as you learn to weave the threads of Hoodoo magic into a life of purpose and empowerment.

My path into the deep currents of Hoodoo began not in a classroom, but through an intuitive recognition of its timeless wisdom—a connection that felt as ancient as the earth itself. As Madame Ophelia, my understanding of Hoodoo is not merely academic; it is a wisdom gleaned from countless cycles observed, seasons turned, and a profound communion with the unseen forces that govern our world. I have spent lifetimes, it feels, immersed in the silent language of root and stone, witnessing how these simple elements hold immense power, not just as ingredients, but as living entities imbued with spiritual resonance. This deep, inherent connection allows me to see the symbolic thread in every action, guiding you not just through spells, but into the very heart of this sacred practice, ensuring you grasp its authentic integrity and rich cultural heritage. My unique perspective, born from generations of silent practice and a profound respect for the ancestral lineage, equips me to be your guide on this journey, unlocking wisdom that resonates from the very earth itself, fostering authentic spiritual growth through simple, yet potent, practices.

Within these pages, you will discover an accessible roadmap to understanding and practicing Hoodoo magic, grounded in respect and practicality. You will learn the true origins of Hoodoo, tracing its journey from African spiritual traditions to its vibrant evolution in the American South, distinguishing it from other magical paths. We will explore the core principles of Hoodoo, revealing how intention, ethical conduct, and personal responsibility are the bedrock of effective magic. You will be guided through essential preparatory practices, mastering techniques for grounding, cleansing, and creating sacred space, ensuring every working is potent and pure. We will delve into nature's abundant toolbox, exploring essential herbs, roots, minerals, and symbolic objects, and critically, how to ethically work with personal concerns to build powerful spiritual connections to your intentions.

Most importantly, you will receive clear, step-by-step instructions for practical magic applications: crafting impenetrable protection spells for your home, body, and spirit; performing potent cleansing and clearing rituals to remove obstacles and stagnant energy; and igniting powerful prosperity and manifestation magic to attract money, opportunity, and success. Finally, you will discover how to cultivate unwavering personal power, designing your own rituals for confidence, influence, and magnetism, enabling you to integrate Hoodoo seamlessly into your modern life for sustained spiritual growth and transformation. This book is an invitation to step into a lineage of profound spiritual resilience and practical wisdom, offered with both reverence and an unwavering commitment to clarity. I've carefully distilled these ancient practices into actionable steps, removing the guesswork so you can confidently apply them to your life today. Embrace this opportunity to forge a deeper connection with the earth, honor the whispers of your ancestors, and unlock the potent magic that resides within you and around you.

Are you ready to discover the authentic power of Hoodoo and transform your life with wisdom that truly works? Let us begin this journey together. As you embark on this path, you will find that Hoodoo is not just a practice but a way of life, a lens through which you can view the world with renewed clarity and purpose. It invites you to engage with the world in a more meaningful way, to see the interconnectedness of all things, and to understand your place within this vast tapestry. The journey you are about to undertake is one of self-discovery and empowerment, where you will learn to harness the energies around you to create the life you desire. The teachings within this book are not just theoretical; they are practical, actionable, and designed to fit seamlessly into your daily routine. You will learn how to incorporate Hoodoo into your life in a way that feels natural and intuitive, allowing you to tap into its power whenever you need it.

Whether you are seeking protection, prosperity, or personal growth, the tools and techniques you will learn here will empower you to take control of your destiny and shape your reality in ways you never thought possible. As you delve deeper into the world of Hoodoo, you will begin to see the world through new eyes. You will notice the subtle signs and symbols that surround you, guiding you on your path and offering insights into the mysteries of the universe. You will learn to trust your intuition and to listen to the whispers of the earth, allowing them to guide you toward your true purpose. This journey is not one you will take alone. You will be guided by the wisdom of those who have walked this path before you, their voices echoing through the ages, offering guidance and support as you navigate the challenges and triumphs of your journey. You will become part of a community of like-minded individuals, all seeking to unlock the secrets of Hoodoo and to harness its power for good.

As you progress through this book, you will find that the teachings of Hoodoo are not just about magic; they are about living a life of integrity, authenticity, and purpose. You will learn to align your actions with your values, to live in harmony with the natural world, and to cultivate a deep sense of gratitude for the blessings in your life. This is the true essence of Hoodoo—a way of being that transcends the mundane and connects you to something greater than yourself. In the pages that follow, you will find a wealth of knowledge and wisdom, carefully curated to provide you with the tools you need to succeed on your journey. You will learn about the history and origins of Hoodoo, its core principles, and the practical applications of its teachings. You will discover how to create powerful rituals and spells, how to work with the energies of the earth, and how to cultivate a deep and abiding connection with the spiritual world.

This book is your guide to unlocking the power of Hoodoo and transforming your life in ways you never thought possible. It is an invitation to step into a world of magic and mystery, to explore the depths of your own potential, and to create a life of abundance, joy, and fulfillment. Are you ready to take the first step on this incredible journey? The path awaits you, and the possibilities are endless. Let us begin.

As you delve into the teachings of Hoodoo, you will find that it is not merely a collection of spells and rituals, but a profound philosophy that encourages you to live with intention and purpose. It is a way of life that honors the interconnectedness of all things and recognizes the power of the individual to effect change in the world. Through the practice of Hoodoo, you will learn to harness the energies of the universe to create the life you desire, to protect yourself and your loved ones, and to manifest your dreams into reality.

The journey you are about to embark on is one of self-discovery and empowerment. It is a journey that will challenge you to look within, to confront your fears and doubts, and to embrace your true potential. As you progress through this book, you will find that the teachings of Hoodoo are not just about magic; they are about living a life of integrity, authenticity, and purpose. You will learn to align your actions with your values, to live in harmony with the natural world, and to cultivate a deep sense of gratitude for the blessings in your life.

In the pages that follow, you will find a wealth of knowledge and wisdom, carefully curated to provide you with the tools you need to succeed on your journey. You will learn about the history and origins of Hoodoo, its core principles, and the practical applications of its teachings. You will discover how to create powerful rituals and spells, how to work with the energies of the earth, and how to cultivate a deep and abiding connection with the spiritual world.

This book is your guide to unlocking the power of Hoodoo and transforming your life in ways you never thought possible. It is an invitation to step into a world of magic and mystery, to explore the depths of your own potential, and to create a life of abundance, joy, and fulfillment. Are you ready to take the first step on this incredible journey? The path awaits you, and the possibilities are endless. Let us begin.

Chapter One

What Is Hoodoo: Understanding African American Folk Magic and Its Living Roots

The Origins of Hoodoo: A Journey from Africa to America

African Spiritual Foundations

hen enslaved Africans stepped onto American soil, they carried no possessions—but something far more enduring. They brought memories of sacred rivers, protective spirits who walked alongside the living, and the profound understanding that every root, every stone, every ancestor held power. These weren't abstract philosophies recorded in dusty texts. They were **lived spiritual practices**, woven into daily existence as naturally as breathing.

African spiritual traditions operated on a fundamentally different principle than the religious structures imposed by enslavers. There was no separation between the sacred and the mundane, no distant deity requiring elaborate intermediaries. Instead, spirituality meant *direct relationship*—with ancestors who remained active participants in family life, with natural forces that responded to respectful petition, with a living world thick with meaning and reciprocity.

Community ritual formed the heartbeat of this worldview. Healing wasn't a solitary act but a collective ceremony drawing upon shared energy and ancestral wisdom. Protection didn't come from passive prayer alone but from deliberate work with herbs, charged objects, and focused intention. When someone needed help, the community gathered, creating a spiritual network stronger than any individual effort.

Ancestor veneration provided the foundation for everything else.

The dead weren't gone—they were elevated, transformed into powerful allies who could intervene on behalf of the living. Maintaining relationship with them wasn't optional sentimentality but essential spiritual maintenance, ensuring protection and guidance flowed between worlds.

These practices didn't die in the Middle Passage or on plantation soil. They adapted, merged, and persisted with remarkable tenacity. What emerged—what we now call Hoodoo—carries these African roots forward, maintaining that essential understanding: **power resides in relationship, in nature, in community, and in the unbroken line connecting us to those who came before**.

The Transatlantic Transformation

The transatlantic slave trade didn't just transport human bodies across an ocean. It attempted to sever souls from their spiritual homelands, to break the sacred bonds connecting people to ancestors, to land, to the divine forces that had sustained their communities for countless generations. Yet spiritual traditions proved far more resilient than those who sought to destroy them could ever imagine.

Enslaved Africans arrived in the Americas carrying no possessions, but they carried something far more durable than material goods: **memory**. They remembered how to speak to ancestors, how to work with plant spirits, how to call upon protective forces. They remembered that certain leaves healed, that crossroads held power, that water carried prayers. These memories, passed mouth to ear in whispered instruction, became the seeds of Hoodoo's survival.

The brutality of enslavement demanded innovation.

Traditional practices had to adapt to new landscapes where familiar plants didn't grow, where gathering for ceremonies meant risking death, where maintaining spiritual knowledge required absolute secrecy. African spiritual frameworks—particularly West and Central African traditions emphasizing ancestor veneration, natural forces, and practical intervention—encountered unfamiliar American plants, absorbed Native American botanical wisdom, and even incorporated European grimoire techniques when useful. This wasn't cultural dilution. It was **strategic transformation**, taking whatever tools proved effective and integrating them into an African spiritual foundation that remained unshakeable at its core.

What emerged was a tradition designed for survival under impossible circumstances. Hoodoo became the spiritual practice of people who needed protection from those who claimed to own them, who required healing when no doctor would treat them, who sought justice in a system built to deny them humanity itself. Every root gathered, every candle dressed, every protective charm hidden above a doorway represented an act of resistance—a refusal to surrender spiritual autonomy even when everything else had been stolen.

Syncretism in the American South

In the American South, Hoodoo transformed into something entirely new—a syncretic practice born from necessity and resilience. Enslaved Africans carried memories of their spiritual traditions across the Middle Passage, but they couldn't practice them unchanged. The brutal conditions of slavery demanded adaptation, and Hoodoo emerged as a creative fusion of **African spiritual knowledge, Native American**

herbalism, and European folk magic (Hazzard-Donald, 2013).. This wasn't dilution of the original traditions. This was survival through synthesis, creating a powerful system of protection, healing, and resistance under impossible circumstances.

The blending happened organically, through shared knowledge and desperate need. Enslaved Africans worked alongside Indigenous peoples in some regions and observed European folk practices in others. They recognized useful techniques and incorporated them, weaving together a magical framework that drew strength from multiple sources while maintaining its distinctly African spiritual foundation. Hoodoo practitioners learned which local roots and herbs could substitute for African plants they could no longer access. They discovered that certain Native American cleansing methods aligned perfectly with African purification rituals. They even camouflaged their work within Christian symbolism when necessary, using Psalms and biblical imagery as protective cover (Dorsey, 2022; Yronwode, n.d.).

This adaptive brilliance allowed African spiritual practices to survive when they otherwise would have been stamped out completely.

What emerged wasn't just magical technique—it was **cultural survival and community cohesion** manifested through spiritual practice. Hoodoo became the thread connecting people to their ancestors, their heritage, and each other, even as everything else was stripped away.

• • •

Distinguishing Hoodoo from Other Magical Traditions

Cultural Roots and Influences

Hoodoo works because it responds to life's immediate demands. When a practitioner lights a candle dressed with protective oil, she's not preparing for some distant spiritual outcome—she's claiming safety right now. When roots are carried in a mojo bag for prosperity, the work addresses today's rent, tomorrow's opportunity, this week's financial crisis. Other magical systems often emphasize spiritual development as the primary goal, with practical results arriving as welcome byproducts of inner transformation. **Hoodoo reverses that equation entirely.**

The tradition emerged from people who couldn't afford to wait for enlightenment.

They needed protection from very real threats. They required healing when medical care was denied. They sought love, justice, and prosperity within systems designed to withhold all three (Chireau, 2003). Hoodoo answered with *methods*—specific techniques producing tangible outcomes. A woman facing eviction didn't need mystical philosophy; she needed the exact combination of roots, prayers, and actions that would keep her family housed. A man confronting workplace injustice required protection strong enough to hold against physical danger, not abstract meditations on universal love.

This practicality extends to **how Hoodoo understands spiritual power itself.** Many traditions position practitioners as supplicants requesting divine intervention from distant deities or channeling energies through complex hierarchical systems. Hoodoo recognizes ancestors as intimately involved family members, natural forces as responsive partners, and spiritual power as something humans can direct through proper knowledge and respectful relationship. You don't beg—you work. You don't simply hope—you act with precision, combining the right roots with the right words at the right time, trusting methods proven across generations.

Consider two practitioners addressing the same problem: unwanted attention from a harmful person. One tradition might prescribe months of meditation to transmute the negativity through inner work, raising vibration until the threat simply dissolves. **The Hoodoo practitioner gathers hot foot powder, lays it where the person will**

walk, and watches them leave—often within days. Both approaches have validity within their systems, but only one was designed for people whose survival depended on immediate, measurable results.

This directness makes Hoodoo particularly suited for modern seekers overwhelmed by spiritual practices promising everything while delivering vague reassurances. The tradition doesn't ask you to transcend your problems; it gives you tools to solve them.

Philosophical and Practical Differences

During the Great Migration, countless African Americans moving from the rural South to industrial cities faced brutal discrimination and crushing economic hardship. When a factory worker dealt with an abusive foreman, or when a domestic worker needed protection from exploitation, Hoodoo offered something other traditions could not: immediate, practical power. A woman might visit her grandmother or a trusted rootworker, not for elaborate ceremony, but for a solution she could carry in her pocket.

The remedy was direct. A small flannel bag, filled with **High John the Conqueror** root for personal strength and a silver dime for prosperity, became her shield. She dressed it with oil each morning, spoke her intention over it—clear words about respect, fair treatment, or the removal of obstacles—and carried it to work. This wasn't mysticism for its own sake. This was **survival magic**, rooted in the understanding that spiritual work must produce real-world results.

Other magical traditions might require months of study, complex symbolism, or initiation into esoteric orders. Hoodoo asks different questions: What do you need? What will work? How can you do this today, with what you have, to change your circumstances right now?

This pragmatic philosophy distinguishes Hoodoo from practices that emphasize ritual purity, hierarchical knowledge, or spiritual advancement as an end in itself. Hoodoo emerged from communities where survival depended on results, not theory. The tradition honors **personal experience** over prescribed dogma, **intention** over elaborate performance, and **community wisdom** over solitary enlightenment. When you work Hoodoo, you work with the understanding that your ancestors needed magic that functioned in the real world—and so do you.

This is why Hoodoo feels accessible even to beginners. You don't need years of preparation to speak your truth over a candle or carry a protective charm. You need clear intention, respect for the practice, and the willingness to act. The power is already yours; Hoodoo simply shows you how to use it.

• • •

The Relevance of Hoodoo Today: Practical Magic in Modern Life

Modern Applications of Hoodoo

Morning coffee becomes protection when you speak a blessing over the cup before drinking. Not theatrical incantations—just your clear intention that the warmth filling your body also fills you with spiritual strength for the day ahead. Stir clockwise three times while naming what you're calling in: clarity, protection, focus. This transforms a mundane act into spiritual fortification.

Keep a small dish of salt by your front door. When you leave for work, touch it briefly and acknowledge that negativity stops at the threshold. When you return home stressed, touch it again and consciously release what doesn't serve you before entering your sanctuary. You've just created a simple threshold protection that requires no elaborate setup, no special timing, just consistent practice.

Your evening shower already cleanses your body. **Make it cleanse your spirit too** by visualizing the water carrying away frustrations, anxieties, and external energies that accumulated during the day. Watch them spiral down the drain. Add a handful of salt once weekly for deeper clearing. Practical magic doesn't require separate rituals—it infuses the routines you already maintain.

Carry protection in your pocket. A silver dime, three bay leaves, or a small piece of pyrite slipped into your bag or wallet creates a mobile shield. No elaborate preparation necessary at first—your intention activates the object. Touch it when entering difficult situations, silently affirming your boundary: *"I am protected. Negativity cannot root here."*

Before important conversations, meetings, or confrontations, take thirty seconds to ground yourself. Place both feet firmly on the floor, breathe deeply three times, and feel your connection to the earth beneath the building. This isn't metaphorical—you're literally stabilizing your energy field through physical awareness. Hoodoo recognizes that **spiritual power flows through your body**, not around it.

Start here, with what you already do. Magic isn't added on top of life—it's woven through it.

Cultural Continuity and Evolution

Hoodoo survived centuries of upheaval because it adapted without abandoning its essence. When African spiritual practices met the realities of the American South, practitioners didn't simply preserve old ways unchanged—they evolved them. They incorporated local herbs when African ones weren't available, wove Christian prayers into older invocations when necessary for survival, and developed new techniques for new challenges while maintaining the core principles that made their magic work.

This adaptability remains Hoodoo's greatest strength. **The tradition honors its roots while growing new branches.** You're not betraying authenticity when you light a candle in your apartment instead of at a crossroads, or when you use tap water instead of river water, or when you adapt a protection ritual to fit your lunch break. You're doing exactly what generations before you did—working the magic that your circumstances allow.

What never changes? **Intention. Respect. Connection to ancestry. The understanding that your actions carry spiritual weight.** These principles remain constant whether you're working in 1820 or 2024, in a rural cabin or a city studio, with traditional roots or modern substitutes.

Modern Hoodoo practitioners face different obstacles than their ancestors—not enslavement, but disconnection. Not physical danger, but spiritual overwhelm. Not lack of materials, but too many choices and conflicting information. Yet the magic still works because human needs haven't fundamentally changed. We still require protection, still seek prosperity, still need to clear away what harms us and draw close what helps.

The tradition's relevance lies precisely in this tension between honoring what was and serving what is. When you practice Hoodoo today, you participate in an unbroken lineage of adaptation—one that trusts you to carry forward both the letter and the spirit of this work.

Empowerment through Practical Magic

You now understand what Hoodoo *is*—folk magic rooted in African American spiritual tradition, built from necessity and survival (Wikipedia, n.d.). (Original Botanica, 2025). (Crescent City Conjure, 2025). (aromaG's Botanica, 2025). You've seen how it survived by adapting without losing its soul. And you recognize that the same principles that guided practitioners through impossible circumstances still speak to the challenges you face right now.

This is magic that meets you where you are.

It doesn't demand years of study before your first working. It doesn't require you to source rare ingredients from distant lands or master complex rituals before addressing the problem keeping you awake tonight. Hoodoo asks for your clear intention, your respectful approach, and your willingness to act with the materials and knowledge available to you. The tradition survived precisely because it worked for real people facing real problems—and it continues working for the same reason.

What you've gained from understanding Hoodoo's living roots isn't just historical appreciation. You've received permission to claim this practice as your own, to trust that your apartment altar holds the same spiritual weight as a rural cabin's hearth, that your lunch-break candle work carries authentic power, that your modern needs deserve the same magical attention your ancestors gave theirs. **The lineage doesn't demand perfection. It asks for sincerity.**

Where does this leave you?

Standing at the threshold between understanding and doing. You know *what* Hoodoo is and *why* it matters. But knowing about protective oils and mojo bags means nothing if they remain abstract concepts. The next step moves from theory into your hands—literally. You'll need to understand the actual tools practitioners use, the materials that transform intention into manifestation, the physical ingredients that bridge the spiritual and material worlds. Herbs, roots, minerals, oils, candles, personal concerns—each carries specific power when used with knowledge and respect.

These aren't symbols. They're the working components of your practice, waiting to be understood and employed.

Chapter Two

The History and Heart of Hoodoo: From Africa to America to Your Life Today

From African Roots: The Birthplace of Hoodoo

Ancestral Traditions and Beliefs

Before enslaved Africans touched American soil, they carried gods in their breath. The Yoruba people venerated *Orisha*—powerful spirits embodying natural forces like rivers, thunder, and iron. The Bakongo traced sacred cosmograms in dirt, marking the boundary between living and dead, honoring *Nkisi* spirits housed in carved figures and bundled cloth. Across West and Central Africa, spiritual power wasn't confined to temples or priests. It lived in every tree offering shelter, every crossroads where paths diverged, every river providing water.

These weren't religions in the European sense—no single holy book, no uniform doctrine stretching across regions. African spirituality flowed through daily life like water through cupped hands, taking the shape it needed. Your grandmother knew which leaves calmed fever. The village elder understood when to appease restless ancestors. Community healers worked directly with plant spirits, not because they'd studied theology but because the knowledge passed through their lineage like eye color or bone structure.

Ancestral reverence formed the bedrock. Your dead weren't gone—they watched, guided, and intervened. You fed them, spoke to them, sought their blessing before major decisions. Nature held intelligence: certain trees possessed wisdom, specific stones carried protection, particular roots opened doors between worlds. When you needed help, you didn't petition distant deities through intermediaries. You built relationship. You offered respect. You learned which spirit answered which need, then worked together toward solutions.

This wasn't faith requiring belief without evidence. It was practical partnership with forces proving themselves useful, generation after generation.

Cultural Syncretism and Survival

When slavers dragged Africans across the ocean, they tried to erase everything—language, family, name, gods. They failed. Spiritual memory survives where physical possessions cannot.

Enslaved people arrived in a landscape filled with unfamiliar plants, hostile laws, and forced proximity to Native Americans who knew this land intimately and Europeans who carried their own grimoire traditions. Survival demanded adaptation. You couldn't openly worship Yoruba deities under the master's watchful eye, but you could praise Catholic saints bearing suspicious resemblance to those same Orisha. You couldn't access African herbs, but Indigenous communities—such as the Cherokee—generously shared knowledge of local plants and their medicinal uses, teaching which American roots carried similar powers. When European spell books mentioned biblical psalms for protection, you absorbed that knowledge too, weaving it into your existing framework.

Cultural syncretism describes this blending—but the word sounds too academic for what actually happened. This wasn't graduate students comparing religions in comfortable libraries. This was life-or-death improvisation, ancestors whispering instructions through dreams while you pretended to pray Christian prayers, hands secretly shaping remembered gestures beneath lowered heads. The fusion of African spiritual foundations with Native American plant wisdom and European folk magic created something stronger than any single tradition alone. Hoodoo became a living testament to resilience, proving that sacred knowledge adapts without surrendering its soul.

Transmitting Traditions Through Generations

You can burn every book. Enslavers understood this, which is why literacy remained illegal for generations. But you cannot burn memory carried in the body, stories told at night, knowledge transferred through hands teaching younger hands to work roots, through voices low enough that white ears couldn't catch the instructions.

Oral tradition became Hoodoo's lifeline. Grandmothers taught granddaughters while cooking, while washing, while working fields—times when gathering looked innocent. The knowledge passed through recipes for poultices and tinctures that served as both medicine and spiritual aid, through spirituals that carried coded instructions for freedom or protection, through stories like those of Br'er Rabbit, which subtly taught resilience and resourcefulness with local plants. Nothing got written down because paper could be confiscated and used as evidence. Everything lived in carefully guarded memory, protected through repetition and relationship.

Community leaders—root workers, conjure doctors, wise women—became living libraries. They held generations of accumulated wisdom, tested methods, warnings about what worked and what failed. You didn't learn from books; you learned from someone who learned from someone who learned from someone who survived.

This matters now because you're continuing that chain. When you light a candle for protection or carry blessed roots, you're using techniques preserved by people who risked everything to remember. They couldn't let slavery erase their spiritual power, so they hid it in plain sight, disguised as superstition, tucked into folklore, embedded in everyday actions that looked harmless to outsiders but carried **profound intention** for those who understood.

That preservation wasn't passive—it required constant, conscious effort across generations who knew these practices meant survival, dignity, and connection to something enslavers could never touch.

• • •

Survival and Adaptation: Hoodoo in the American South

Cultural Amalgamation and Syncretism

Hoodoo survived precisely because enslaved Africans refused to let it die purely intact. When circumstance forbids preserving something whole, you preserve what matters most—and that requires transformation.

African ancestors arrived knowing particular plants held spiritual power. But those plants didn't grow in American soil. So they observed which Native peoples were thriving, which herbs they used, what local roots carried medicine. **Cherokee knowledge of yellowroot**, often used for medicinal and cleansing purposes, merged with remembered uses for African bitter roots (Moerman, 1998). Enslaved workers traded plant wisdom with Indigenous peoples who understood what it meant to have your world remade by violence. This exchange wasn't theft—it was survival education between peoples who recognized kindred need.

European influences entered differently. Slaveholders imposed Christianity, expecting complete spiritual surrender. Instead, practitioners found workable pieces. The **Book of Psalms** offered ready-made protection prayers in the master's own language—reciting them looked like pious conversion while actually fueling conjure work (Anderson, 2008). Catholic saint imagery provided convenient masks: lighting a candle to **Saint Peter**, known as the keeper of keys and gates, could represent seeking spiritual access to opportunities or overcoming blockages. Moses became a hoodoo man himself—didn't he work wonders with a staff and outwit Pharaoh's magicians?

The result wasn't dilution. It was creative resistance forged under impossible conditions. You worked with what grew where you stood, spoke in words that wouldn't get you killed, and preserved the essential truth: *spiritual power remains accessible to those who know how to reach it, regardless of what you must call it aloud.*

Strategies of Resistance and Survival

Sharla Fett's research uncovered how enslaved women working as healers systematically concealed spiritual practice within permitted medical care. **Midwives and herbalists** moved through plantations with legitimate access to birthing rooms, sick quarters, and private spaces where other enslaved people gathered—places where root work could happen under the guise of tending bodies. A woman brewing herbs for fever might simultaneously be preparing a protective wash. Birth attendants speaking prayers over laboring mothers invoked ancestors alongside any Christian saints masters expected to hear named (Fett, 2002).

This wasn't deception—it was strategic survival.

Planters depended on these healers, creating space practitioners used brilliantly. When slaveholders saw conjure as harmless superstition, that dismissal became protective cover. *Let them think us simple*, the logic went, *while we work what actually matters*. Frederick Douglass himself wrote about fearing an enslaver named Covey less after carrying a protective root given by an older man, describing how that small act of spiritual resistance fundamentally shifted his psychological relationship to his own oppression

(Douglass, 1845). The root might have been simple—but the **reclaimed sense of power** it represented was anything but.

Conjure doctors gained influence that transcended their legal status as property. They settled disputes, identified thieves through divination, protected people from cruelty both physical and spiritual. This created an entire parallel authority structure slaveholders couldn't fully see or control. Community members sought these practitioners not from superstition but from practical need—and from profound hunger for spaces where their own wisdom, their own power, their own judgment actually mattered.

Hoodoo's covert practice established patterns still visible today: knowledge shared carefully within trusted relationships, work done privately, results spoken about cautiously. What began as necessary secrecy became protective tradition, ensuring practices passed to those who'd respect rather than exploit them.

Transformation into a Southern Tradition

After Emancipation, many formerly enslaved practitioners openly claimed titles their communities had long recognized privately. **Root doctors, conjurers, and two-headed workers** became visible fixtures of Southern life, consulted across racial lines for needs unmet by conventional medicine or religion. White Southerners, publicly dismissive of conjure as slave superstition, quietly sought Black root workers for love problems, business troubles, and incurable illnesses.

This created precarious dynamics.

Practitioners gained economic independence and community respect, but visibility brought danger. Local success attracted clients and suspicion. While white clients often brought protection and income when satisfied, disappointing results or perceived threats to the white supremacist order could turn those same clients into accusers. Root workers learned to read power carefully, discerning which requests to accept, which clients posed more risk than reward, and when a flourishing practice became a target.

Hoodoo adapted to Southern ecosystems with remarkable specificity. Practitioners substituted local plants, such as **devil's shoestring** for African roots, and southern graveyard dirt for ancestral soil from specific regions. The Mississippi River gained spiritual significance, mirroring West African sacred waterways, especially in the development of traditions like New Orleans Voodoo. Crossroads in the rural South became sites where the veil thinned, for burying workings or meeting spirits at midnight, drawing from the Kongo cosmogram. (Long, 2023)

This environmental adaptation meant Hoodoo became inseparable from Southern identity itself—not imported practice but living tradition grown from this specific soil.

Contemporary Relevance and Legacy

When Hoodoo took root in Southern soil, it didn't just survive—it transformed into a living testament to creativity under pressure. The practices you learn today carry within them generations of adaptation, resistance, and profound spiritual resilience.

Understanding this legacy matters because **authentic Hoodoo practice requires knowing where the power comes from**. When you light a candle for protection or prepare a spiritual bath, you're participating in a tradition that sustained people through unimaginable hardship. These weren't theoretical exercises; they were lifelines. Rootworkers passed down practical knowledge that addressed real needs: safety from harm, justice when legal systems failed, healing when medicine was denied, and hope when circumstances seemed hopeless. This practical foundation is why Hoodoo remains so effective today—it was forged in necessity and refined through lived experience.

The Southern landscape itself became part of the practice. **Local roots, herbs, and minerals were incorporated**, blending African spiritual knowledge with what the land offered. This wasn't dilution; it was innovation born from deep observation and spiritual attunement.

Today, when you honor this history, you're not just performing rituals—you're connecting to a current of power that flows from ancestors who refused to let their spirits be broken. Their legacy lives in every mojo bag you create, every floor wash you prepare, every intention you set with focused will.

• • •

Bringing History to Practice: The Relevance of Tradition Today

Connecting Past to Present

Start simple: **light a candle with intention this week.** Not someday when conditions feel perfect—tonight, tomorrow morning, whenever you read this. Use any candle you have. White works for general blessing, but a kitchen taper or birthday candle honors the tradition just as well. Hoodoo respects what's available.

Before lighting it, hold the candle between your palms. Feel its weight. *Speak your need* directly—protection for your home, clarity about a decision, strength to handle what tomorrow brings. Don't perform or try to sound mystical. Your ancestors understood plain speech.

Light the candle and let it burn while you're nearby. Watch the flame for a few minutes if you can. This isn't passive meditation; you're establishing relationship between your intention and the element carrying it forward.

Next, identify three plants already in your space. Basil from the kitchen cabinet. The mint growing wild near your building. Rosemary purchased for cooking but sitting untouched. **Research one traditional use for each**—not five hours of internet rabbit holes, just fifteen minutes of focused reading about their protective or cleansing properties in folk practice. Carolyn Morrow Long's work or Catherine Yronwode's practical guides offer solid starting points. (Yronwode, 2002)

By week's end, brew a simple wash: boil water, steep one of those herbs, let it cool. Wipe down your front doorframe with the strained liquid, moving from top to bottom. You're establishing threshold protection using knowledge you now possess, not someday expertise you're still waiting to acquire.

Cultural Heritage in Modern Practice

Understanding where Hoodoo comes from isn't just about history—it's about deepening the power of your practice. When you recognize the African ancestors who preserved these traditions through unimaginable hardship, when you honor the Native American herbalists who shared their plant wisdom, and when you acknowledge the European influences that wove into the fabric of Southern folk magic (Virginia & Rook, 2024), you're doing more than learning facts. You're stepping into a living lineage that strengthens every spell you cast.

Cultural respect begins with knowledge. Before you light your first candle or mix your first floor wash, take time to understand what these practices meant to the people who created them. Protection spells weren't just superstition—they were survival tools. Prosperity work wasn't greed—it was claiming dignity in a system designed to deny it. Ancestor veneration wasn't nostalgia—it was maintaining connection to wisdom that couldn't be written down or stolen away. When you approach Hoodoo with this awareness, your intentions carry weight. Your rituals resonate with authenticity.

Incorporating cultural elements respectfully means *learning the why* behind the what. Don't just use High John the Conqueror root because it's powerful—understand its symbolism of overcoming oppression and reclaiming personal power. Don't just pour out libations because it's traditional—recognize this as honoring the ancestors whose strength flows through your practice. When you connect ritual actions to their cultural meanings, you transform mechanical steps into sacred work.

This genuine connection transforms everything. Your magic becomes conversation with tradition, not just procedure. You grow roots that anchor and sustain your spiritual path for years to come.

Practical Applications Today

Hoodoo thrives when it moves beyond history books and into your hands, your kitchen, your morning routine. The practices your ancestors carried across oceans aren't museum pieces—they're **living tools** designed to address the same fundamental needs you face today: protection from harm, clarity in confusion, abundance where there's lack.

Consider the simple **spiritual bath**. Enslaved people used what they had—salt, herbs from the woods, prayers whispered in darkness—to cleanse away oppression's weight and reclaim their power (Hoodoo & Herbal Spiritual Baths, 2025; Wikipedia, 2026). You can draw that same bath tonight. Add hyssop for purification, sea salt to clear negativity, speak your intention over the water. The ritual adapts to your apartment bathroom or farmhouse tub, but its *essence* remains unchanged: washing away what diminishes you, emerging renewed.

Protection work translates especially well to modern life. Your ancestors protected their homes with red brick dust swept across thresholds (aromaG's Botanica, 2025; Cajun Conjuror, n.d.); you can do the same, or substitute cayenne pepper if brick dust proves hard to find. The *principle* matters more than perfect replication—you're creating a barrier against negative energy, marking your space as sacred and secure.

Start small. Choose one traditional practice that speaks to your current need. Learn its history, understand its purpose, then **make it yours**. Carry a mojo bag for confidence before important meetings. Dress candles for prosperity on new moons. Speak to your ancestors each morning, even if it's just "Good morning, I remember you."

This isn't about performing museum-quality reconstructions. It's about letting **ancestral wisdom breathe** through your contemporary challenges, proving once again that Hoodoo works precisely because it bends without breaking, adapts without forgetting, and serves each generation's needs while honoring every generation's sacrifice.

Chapter Three

Core Principles of Hoodoo: How Folk Magic Works and Why Intention Matters

The Heart of Hoodoo: Embracing Intention and Connection

Intention as Magical Catalyst

You can carry the most expensive crystal on earth, recite every prayer perfectly, and still watch your work fail if your **intention is cloudy**. A woman once told me she'd performed a protection ritual three times without results. When I asked what she was protecting against, she paused. "Bad things, I guess?" That vagueness is why her work collapsed before it began.

Hoodoo doesn't run on hope or wishing. It runs on *directed spiritual force*, and that force flows through one channel: your intention. Before your hands ever touch a candle or reach for salt, your mind must know exactly what you're asking the spirits and roots to accomplish. Not a general feeling. Not a broad theme. A specific outcome you could describe to someone in one clear sentence.

When practitioners from generations past worked protection, they named the threat—a specific person, a known danger, a particular crossroads after dark. When they worked for money, they saw the exact bill coming due, the job interview on Tuesday, the hands exchanging payment. This precision transformed simple materials into spiritual artillery.

Think of intention as the address on a letter.

You wouldn't mail an envelope marked "somewhere nice"—it would never arrive. Yet people approach Hoodoo work this way constantly, wondering why their energy scatters like dust. Ancestors who worked roots under threat of violence couldn't afford scattered energy. They needed results, which meant they needed clarity that cut like a blade through fog.

Setting intention isn't meditation or centering yourself for twenty minutes. It's the moment before action when you state your purpose so clearly that the spirits can't misunderstand and your own doubt can't interfere. You don't need perfect words. You need **honest specificity**.

Before lighting that first candle, ask yourself: What changes when this work succeeds? If you can't answer in concrete terms—not feelings, but facts—your intention needs sharpening. The roots and rituals will meet you exactly where your clarity ends.

Connecting with Natural Forces

Clarity alone won't move your work forward if you're disconnected from the forces that actually power it. Hoodoo isn't performed in a vacuum—it's a **partnership with the natural world**, an exchange between your focused will and the intelligence embedded in roots, minerals, water, and earth itself.

Every element you work with carries its own signature, its own medicine. High John root doesn't just symbolize strength—it *holds* strength, accumulated through seasons of growth in specific soil, shaped by rain and sun into a physical vessel of resilience. When you carry that root in your pocket, you're not performing theater. You're allying yourself with something that exists independent of your belief, something practitioners have verified through generations of results.

This relationship requires attention, not reverence for its own sake. You need to understand what you're asking from these materials and why they can deliver. Salt draws from ancient oceans and purifies because it preserves, because it creates environments where corruption can't survive. Sulfur repels because its smell itself drives things away—the spiritual logic mirrors the physical reality. Graveyard dirt connects you to the dead because it literally holds their remains, making it a direct line to ancestral power when gathered with respect and proper payment.

Most people approach Hoodoo like a recipe: add ingredients, follow steps, expect results.

But roots and minerals aren't inert components waiting for your activation. They're active forces you're entering into relationship with, and that relationship works best when you've attuned yourself to the rhythms they follow. Gather herbs on certain moon phases not because mystical energy peaks then, but because traditional agricultural wisdom has long recognized lunar influences on plant vitality and growth patterns. Work water magic near moving rivers because flowing water **carries and cleanses** in ways stagnant water can't. These aren't arbitrary rules—they're observations about how natural forces operate, codified by people whose survival depended on accuracy.

When you stop treating nature as backdrop and start recognizing it as your primary collaborator, the work changes completely.

Building Spiritual Relationships

Working with nature gets you halfway there. Working with your ancestors and spiritual allies completes the circuit.

Most people struggling with Hoodoo are trying to do everything alone, relying only on their individual will to power protection spells or manifestation work. They wonder why the work feels hollow, why candles burn but nothing shifts. The answer is simple: **Hoodoo has always been a collective practice**, drawing power from relationships that extend beyond the living (Hazzard-Donald, 2013). Your grandmothers who walked this path before you, the spirits who align with your purpose, the ancestors whose blood runs in your veins—these aren't optional additions to your practice. They're the foundation.

When you light a candle asking for protection without acknowledging the ancestors who survived impossible circumstances to keep you here, you're rejecting the strongest allies available to you. When you work for prosperity without building relationship with spirits who've helped countless practitioners before you, you're choosing the hardest possible route.

This isn't about elaborate ritual or theatrical devotion. It's about recognition: you're not the first person to face this problem, and the wisdom accumulated by those who came before is *accessible* if you're willing to reach for it. Building these relationships starts with consistency, not perfection. A glass of water refreshed weekly on your ancestor altar matters more than occasional elaborate offerings. Speaking to them regularly—telling them your struggles, asking for guidance, updating them on your life—creates the kind of ongoing connection that makes them invested in your success. They're not distant cosmic forces requiring appeasement. They're your people, and most of them want to see you thrive.

The spiritual allies you work with—whether that's spirits attached to specific roots, guardian spirits, or helpful forces you've developed relationships with over time—operate on similar principles. They respond to **respect, clear communication, and fair exchange**. You give them offerings that honor their nature. They lend you their particular strengths when your work aligns with their interests. (Hazzard-Donald, 2013)

When you stop trying to do everything through raw personal effort and start leveraging these spiritual partnerships, the work becomes exponentially more effective.

• • •

Respecting Spiritual Laws: The Ethical Backbone of Magic

Understanding Spiritual Laws

Hoodoo operates within spiritual laws as real as gravity, invisible forces that don't require your belief but will absolutely respond to your actions. Our ancestors understood these laws not through abstract philosophy but through direct observation: certain behaviors produced certain results with the consistency of seeds sprouting in good soil. When practitioners speak of "spiritual laws," we're talking about verifiable patterns observed across generations, principles that governed how power moved through the world long before anyone wrote them down.

The first law centers on reciprocity—what you send out returns to you, amplified by the spiritual forces you've invoked. This isn't karma in some vague cosmic sense. It's mechanics. When you work harmful magic against someone, you're establishing a connection between yourself and destructive energy. That connection runs both ways. The same spiritual current you direct outward creates a channel back to you, and spiritual forces don't distinguish between sender and target once you've opened that pathway. Root workers who specialized in cursing often lived isolated lives, their own work circling back to them in illness, broken relationships, and spiritual contamination that clung like smoke to fabric.

Protection magic, by contrast, strengthens your own boundaries while establishing them for others. The energy pattern reinforces itself constructively.

Some practitioners try circumventing this law by having someone else perform harmful work on their behalf. The law doesn't care about your intermediary. Your intention initiated the action, your desired outcome shapes the working, and spiritual forces recognize the true source regardless of whose hands lit the candle.

The second law demands honesty in your spiritual work. You can't lie to spirits with any more success than you can lie to your own heartbeat. When you tell ancestors you're seeking justice while actually nursing petty revenge, when you claim you need money for survival while planning luxury purchases, when you dress up jealousy as righteous protection—the spirits know. They've watched humans long enough to recognize every self-deception we attempt. Practitioners commonly observe that work rooted in dishonesty produces unstable results. For instance, an individual might perform prosperity rituals, yet the desired abundance remains elusive because the true intent is not for personal growth but to incite jealousy in an ex-partner. The spirits, discerning the underlying motive, do not empower endeavors fueled by spite, regardless of how meticulously the outward actions are performed (Yronwode, 2001). Work rooted in dishonesty damages your relationship with the spiritual allies you'll need for genuine help later.

The third law requires clean spiritual hands before attempting powerful work. You can't effectively protect your home while maintaining active feuds that invite chaos. You can't draw love while harboring resentment that poisons everything you touch. You can't petition for clarity while refusing to examine your own role in ongoing problems.

Think of it as spiritual hygiene—attempting major workings without addressing your own contamination is like performing surgery without washing your hands. The infection spreads.

Balancing Power and Responsibility

Power without accountability creates chaos. Magic responds to intention, but it also answers to balance. When you work Hoodoo, you're not operating in isolation—you're part of an intricate web of energy, ancestry, and consequence. Every spell, every root worked, every candle lit sends ripples through that web.

The question isn't whether you *can* do something.

It's whether you *should*.

Personal power in Hoodoo means more than mastering techniques or memorizing correspondences. It means understanding that your actions carry weight. When you work magic to influence a situation, you're introducing your will into a complex system. That system includes other people's free will, ancestral wisdom, spiritual forces, and the natural order of things. Your responsibility is to honor all of these elements, not just your immediate desires.

Consider a simple example: working magic to draw someone's romantic attention. You have the knowledge.

You have the tools. You could absolutely perform that work. But ethical practice requires you to pause and ask deeper questions. Are you overriding someone's free will? Are you trying to force an outcome that serves only yourself?

Or are you working to open pathways for genuine connection, allowing choice and mutual benefit? The difference between these approaches defines whether your magic operates with integrity.

Hoodoo has always balanced personal empowerment with **community responsibility**. Rootworkers in traditional practice understood they served not just individual clients, but the well-being of entire communities. They knew that magic wielded selfishly or recklessly eventually turns back on the worker. (Original Botanica, 2025; Chesapeake Conjure Society, n.d.; The Queen Po, 2025) (Original Botanica, 2025; Lemon8, 2025)

This isn't superstition—it's spiritual law.

Ethical responsibility in practice means asking yourself three questions before any working:

- Does this align with my deepest values, not just my immediate frustrations?
- Am I respecting the free will and dignity of everyone involved?
- Can I accept full responsibility for whatever consequences emerge?

These questions aren't obstacles to your power. They're the foundation of it. Magic worked with clarity of conscience moves with greater force than magic tangled in justifications and half-truths. When you know your work is righteous, when your intentions are clean, the spirits respond differently. Your ancestors stand behind you.

The work flows.

This doesn't mean you can't work protective magic that turns harm back to its source, or that you must accept mistreatment passively. **Ethical practice isn't weakness**. It's discernment. It's the difference between defending yourself and attacking indiscriminately.

Between seeking justice and seeking revenge. Between working for your highest good and working from your wounded ego.

You hold real power when you practice Hoodoo. Respect it enough to use it wisely.

• • •

Personal Responsibility: Power and Accountability in Practice

Understanding Magical Consequences

Every action you take in Hoodoo sends ripples through both the spiritual and physical worlds. When you light a candle, whisper a prayer, or craft a mojo bag, you set energy into motion—energy that doesn't simply vanish once your ritual ends. It moves outward, touches lives, shifts circumstances, and returns to you in ways both subtle and profound.

This is the weight of **personal responsibility** in magical practice. Understanding that your intentions create real effects means accepting accountability for what you set in motion. If you work a spell to draw love, you must be prepared for the changes that love brings—not just the romance, but the vulnerability, the compromise, the transformation of your daily life. If you perform protection work, you're claiming the power to shield yourself, which also means you're responsible for maintaining that shield and addressing why you needed it in the first place. Magic doesn't operate in a vacuum. It interweaves with your choices, your relationships, and the world around you.

Consider this: when you perform a prosperity spell, you're not just asking for money to appear. You're opening pathways for opportunity, and those pathways require you to walk through them. The spell might bring a job offer, but you must show up for the interview. It might spark a business idea, but you need to take the steps to build it. **Magic works with you, not instead of you.** The spiritual work creates momentum, but your actions in the physical realm determine where that momentum leads.

The same principle applies to how your magic affects others.

When your work involves another person—whether you're drawing them closer, pushing them away, or seeking to influence their actions—you carry responsibility for that impact. Hoodoo doesn't shy away from compelling work or commanding spells, but it demands that you approach such practices with clear eyes and honest intentions. Ask yourself: *Am I acting from genuine need or petty spite? Will this work serve a purpose beyond my ego? Can I live with the consequences if this unfolds in unexpected ways?* These questions aren't meant to paralyze you with doubt. They're meant to sharpen your clarity and strengthen your resolve.

Anticipating consequences means thinking beyond your immediate desire. If you're working to remove an obstacle, consider what might rush in to fill that space. If you're sweetening someone's disposition toward you, reflect on whether you're prepared to nurture that relationship authentically. **Responsible magic requires foresight**—the willingness to look three steps ahead and accept what you find there.

Managing these consequences begins with honesty. When your work creates an outcome you didn't expect, own it. Don't blame the spirits, the ancestors, or the universe. Examine your intention, your execution, and the energy you brought to the work. Then adjust. Hoodoo is a living practice, and living things adapt. If a spell's effects ripple too far or too fast, you can perform cleansing work to calm the waters. If your magic brings change that proves uncomfortable, you can do the inner work needed to meet that change with grace.

This is how power and accountability walk hand in hand. You claim your power by stepping into your magic with confidence and purpose. You honor that power by wielding it with integrity, knowing that every spell, every prayer, every intention you send into the world reflects who you are and who you're becoming. The practice doesn't demand perfection. It demands **consciousness**—a deliberate awareness of what you're doing and why you're doing it, paired with the courage to accept what comes next.

Integrity in Practice

Practicing Hoodoo with integrity means building something that lasts. Every time you choose honesty over self-deception, every pause to examine your intentions before striking that match, you strengthen the foundation beneath your spiritual work. This isn't about achieving impossible moral perfection. It's about approaching your practice with **clear conscience and open hands**, understanding that spirits move most powerfully through practitioners who aren't tangled in their own contradictions.

Cultural respect functions the same way. When you honor the African American roots of this tradition—when you acknowledge the ancestors who preserved these practices through unimaginable hardship, when you use proper names instead of sanitized substitutes—you maintain the integrity of the spiritual current itself. Hoodoo didn't survive centuries of suppression to be stripped of its history and repackaged as generic "folk magic." **The power flows through the lineage**. Respect that lineage, and you access something far stronger than any improvised working could generate alone.

Aligning magical work with personal values isn't restrictive—it's clarifying.

When you know what you stand for, when you've examined your ethics deeply enough to articulate them without hesitation, you can work magic with genuine conviction. You won't waste energy second-guessing yourself after the candle burns down. You won't lie awake wondering if you crossed an invisible line. **Clear values create clean magic**, and clean magic encounters less resistance moving through the world. The spirits recognize practitioners who know themselves, who've done the difficult internal work of defining their boundaries and living by articulated principles.

Community principles matter because Hoodoo has never existed as purely individual practice. Even working alone in your home at midnight, you're part of a tradition extending backward through generations and forward into a future your choices help shape. Your decision to work ethically, to respect the culture, to take full responsibility for your magic's ripple effects—these contribute directly to the tradition's vitality. Every practitioner approaching this work with genuine reverence makes it easier for the next seeker to find authentic guidance. Every person who cuts corners or dismisses the roots makes the path murkier for everyone walking behind them.

You understand now that this practice demands both power and accountability, that you cannot separate magical effectiveness from ethical clarity. You've learned how honesty with yourself and the spirits creates stronger outcomes than elaborate ritual performed with contaminated intentions. What comes next builds directly on this foundation—the practical tools and tangible materials that transform these principles into action, bringing Hoodoo from theory into the details of your daily life.

Chapter Four

Preparing Yourself for Practice: Grounding, Cleansing, and Creating Sacred Space

Grounding Yourself: Establishing a Connection with Earth Energy

Understanding Earth Energy

Most practitioners work too hard and collapse before the real magic even begins.

Grounding isn't theory or abstraction. It's direct physical connection to the earth's stabilizing current—the same energy our ancestors accessed barefoot in Southern soil, tending gardens that fed bodies *and* spirits. When you ground, you're drawing from something fundamentally different than nervous personal energy. Earth energy doesn't fray or scatter. It doesn't spike with anxiety or collapse from exhaustion. This matters because effective rootwork demands a steady spiritual frequency that can hold intention without wavering, channel power without burning out, and maintain clarity when forces start moving.

Without proper grounding, you bring unstable energy to sacred work. You're like a lamp plugged into a failing circuit—flickering, unreliable, potentially dangerous. The spirits notice. Your workings feel that instability and reflect it back as inconsistent results, scattered manifestations, or magic that rebounds unpredictably.

Earth energy functions as both anchor and filter. It stabilizes you when spiritual work opens channels that can overwhelm untrained practitioners. When you're properly grounded, the connection helps regulate your autonomic nervous system toward a more relaxed state, allowing excess energy to dissipate harmlessly into the ground (Chevalier et al., 2012). This simultaneously filters out the mental static—worry, doubt, scattered thoughts—that weakens magical focus the way moisture weakens gunpowder.

Hoodoo practitioners understood this intuitively. They worked dirt between their fingers, planted by moon phases, and recognized soil as living intelligence holding accumulated power from seasons, weather, and everything that grew, died, and returned to earth.

Simple Grounding Techniques

The earth pulses with an ancient rhythm, a steady hum that has sustained life since the first breath of creation. When you ground yourself, you tap into this primordial current, anchoring your spirit in something vast and eternal. Without this connection, your magic floats untethered, like smoke dissipating into nothing. Grounding transforms fleeting intention into rooted power.

Visualization offers the simplest gateway to Earth energy. Stand barefoot if you can, feeling the solid ground beneath you. Close your eyes and imagine roots extending from the soles of your feet, pushing deep into the soil, through layers of clay and stone, reaching down to the molten heart of the world. With each breath, these roots draw up rich, stabilizing energy—dark, fertile, unwavering. Feel it rise through your legs, your spine, your chest, filling every hollow place within you. This is not mere imagination; you are establishing a real energetic exchange, grounding scattered thoughts and emotions into focused presence. Practice this daily, even for just three minutes, and notice how your magic gains weight and substance.

Physical movement deepens what visualization begins.

Walk deliberately, feeling each footfall connect with the earth. Kneel and place your palms flat against the ground, sensing its coolness, its texture, its patient strength. Tend a plant, work soil between your fingers, or stand against a tree with your spine pressed to its bark. These acts are **embodied grounding**—they remind your flesh that you are not separate from nature but woven into its fabric. When your body remembers this truth, your spirit remembers too, and your Hoodoo work gains the solid foundation it requires to manifest real change in your life.

Incorporating Grounding into Rituals

Scattered practice yields scattered results. Grounding transforms magic from something you occasionally remember when life falls apart into something you **embody** every single day.

Begin every ritual with grounding, even the brief ones. Before you light that candle for protection, before you mix that honey jar for sweetening, before you speak a single word of intention—root yourself first. This isn't optional preparation; it's the foundation everything else builds upon. When you ground before working, you shift from someone performing magic to someone channeling it through their entire being. Your words carry more weight. Your intentions land with precision rather than drifting into vague hope. The difference shows up in how quickly your work manifests and how deeply it holds.

Morning grounding sets the tone before the world makes its demands. Stand at your threshold, visualize those roots extending downward, draw up earth energy for thirty seconds. You've just claimed your power.

Evening grounding releases what you've accumulated throughout the day—the frustration, the static, the energetic debris clinging to you from other people's moods and agendas. Place your hands on the ground or floor, imagine all that interference draining away through your roots, returning to the earth that transforms even spiritual garbage into neutral soil. Between workings, ground again. If you cleanse with hyssop, ground afterward. If you petition your ancestors, ground when you step away from their altar. This prevents spiritual vertigo, that unmoored feeling from opening to powerful forces without properly closing the exchange.

Consistency transforms technique into instinct. When grounding becomes automatic, your magic becomes **exponentially** stronger.

. . .

Cleansing and Protecting: Ensuring a Safe and Sacred Environment

The Art of Cleansing

Cleansing is not hygiene—it's spiritual intervention. You're not tidying up. You're actively removing energetic residue that clings to walls, doorways, and corners the way smoke settles into fabric. Every argument, every visitor carrying their troubles through your threshold, every moment of fear or anger you've experienced leaves traces. These accumulations don't dissipate on their own.

Hoodoo treats space as porous, vulnerable to influence from both sides of the veil. Your home absorbs everything that happens within it. Without regular clearing, you're attempting sacred work in contaminated conditions, like trying to brew medicine in a dirty pot. The spirits won't enter polluted space, and your own energy can't rise to its full strength when surrounded by spiritual debris.

Our ancestors understood this with urgent clarity. Enslaved practitioners couldn't afford spaces where negative forces lingered—survival depended on maintaining spiritual integrity under constant threat. They swept doorways at dawn, scrubbed thresholds with salt water, and burned purifying herbs in corners where shadows gathered (Long, 2001). (Chireau, 2003). These weren't quaint customs. They were necessary protection.

Cleansing creates vacancy. It removes what doesn't belong so that what you're calling forward has room to arrive. When you clear a space before setting up an altar or preparing for a working, you're establishing spiritual boundaries as real as locked doors.

This practice becomes even more critical before significant rootwork. Attempting to draw prosperity into a space still holding last month's despair guarantees confusion. The old energy and new intention collide, weakening both. Clean first, then call what you need.

Tools for Protection

The tools you choose for protection aren't random—each carries specific energies that work together to fortify your space. Hoodoo protection relies on **layered defenses**, combining herbs, minerals, and symbolic objects to create barriers that guard against both physical negativity and spiritual intrusion. Understanding these materials and their proper use transforms your home into a sacred sanctuary.

Red brick dust forms your first line of defense. Ground from old red bricks—ideally from structures that witnessed strength rather than tragedy—it creates a threshold spirits find difficult to cross. Sprinkle it across doorways and windowsills, particularly at your front entrance. The rust-colored powder acts as both a visual boundary and an energetic barrier, declaring your space protected territory.

Salt purifies and repels negative energy with remarkable efficiency. Mix it with crushed eggshells to amplify its protective properties, then place small amounts beneath windowsills and in room corners. Sea salt carries the ocean's cleansing power, while table salt works perfectly well when blessed with intention. Replace these mixtures monthly, disposing of the old salt away from your property to carry negativity far from your threshold.

Protective herbs offer targeted spiritual defense. **Rue** breaks hexes and shields against ill will. **Angelica root** invites guardian spirits while repelling harmful influences. **Devil's shoestring** tangles up trouble before it reaches your door. Hang bundles of these herbs above entrances, tuck them into protective mojo bags, or burn them as incense to strengthen your space's spiritual boundaries.

These aren't decorative choices—they're deliberate acts of spiritual fortification that require regular maintenance and clear intention to remain effective.

Rituals for Sacred Space

Consecrating your space transforms protective materials into **activated spiritual infrastructure**. You've placed the red brick dust and salt, hung the herbs—now these passive guardians need deliberate awakening through ritual that binds your intention to their natural properties. Without consecration, you're arranging furniture. With it, you're establishing living boundaries that respond to spiritual threats.

Start by clearing the space completely. Open windows, sweep clockwise from back to front, physically removing dust and debris. This isn't just housework—it's the first gesture of respect toward what you're creating. Burn frankincense or sage, moving through each room while stating your purpose aloud: *"I cleanse this space of all negativity, all interference, all harm."* Your voice carries weight here. The smoke doesn't just smell pleasant; it's carrying your intention into every corner, every shadow, every place where stagnant energy might hide.

Next comes the blessing of your protective materials.

Hold each item—the brick dust container, the salt mixture, the herb bundles—and speak directly to them. Tell the salt what you need it to do. Ask the rue to guard your threshold. This isn't symbolic theater; you're establishing **working agreements** with forces that respond to clear instruction and genuine respect. Some practitioners anoint materials with blessing oil or holy water. Others simply hold them while praying. Choose what resonates, but don't skip this step.

Walk your perimeter counterclockwise to banish, then clockwise to seal. As you move, visualize brilliant white or blue light forming an unbreakable barrier at every threshold, every corner, every vulnerable point. Place your protected salt and brick dust with intention, not habit. Consecration fails when you rush through it like a chore, when your mind wanders to grocery lists, when you're performing steps without *meaning* them.

The work demands presence. If you notice your attention drifting, stop. Ground yourself again. Begin where you left off with renewed focus. Reconsecrate monthly, or whenever your space feels spiritually compromised—protection degrades through spiritual wear just as physical barriers weather through time.

Maintaining Energetic Boundaries

Dedicate a regular time, like Sunday, to walk your space. Sprinkle fresh salt water along thresholds, checking physical protections. Replace depleted elements like brick dust or herb bundles immediately. This is practical attention, much like checking door locks, not paranoia.

Notice your space's *energetic temperature*. Does the air feel clear or heavy upon entry, or do certain corners suddenly feel uncomfortable? Trust these sensations as data.

A room that now makes your shoulders tense needs immediate attention: burn cleansing herbs, refresh salt lines, and speak your boundaries aloud with renewed force. After conflict, illness, or draining visitors, perform emergency cleansing immediately. Open windows, sweep physically, then energetically with a besom or hands. Refresh all protective layers.

Keep essential supplies ready: extra salt, dried herbs, matches, and incense easily accessible. Maintenance fails when it requires too much effort; make it effortless by being prepared. Ancestral wisdom teaches that spiritual protection requires consistent attention, like tending crops or tools. Neglect invites disaster; attention preserves power. Your protected space strengthens through **repetition and relationship**, each session deepening its capacity to hold what you need and repel threats.

• • •

Mindset for Magic: Cultivating Focus and Intention

Embracing Intentionality

Clarifying intention begins with a direct confrontation: what exactly do you want? Not what you think you should want, nor vague improvement, but the specific outcome for your effort. Hoodoo work fails most often not from incorrect materials or improper timing but from muddy intention—spiritual energy scatters when you haven't decided where it's going.

Write your desire in one sentence. Not three paragraphs of context, not conditional clauses, not "maybe" or "if possible." One declarative sentence: "I am surrounded by protective energy that shields me from harm" or "I will secure employment by month's end." Read it aloud. Does it sound true? Does your body recognize it as real? If doubt rises when you speak it, your intention needs sharpening—the spirit world responds to certainty, not wishful thinking.

Now place your hand over your heart and repeat that sentence three times, feeling each word settle into your chest. This is not performance. This is alignment—bringing your physical body, your conscious mind, and your spiritual will into the same current. When all three move together, your magic stops being hope and becomes direction.

Test your intention by asking: *What would change if this manifested tomorrow?* If you can't answer clearly, you haven't yet found the true desire beneath the surface want. Keep digging. The root of your intention lives deeper than your first answer.

Once your intention rings clear—once you can state it without hedging and feel it without flinching—you've given your spiritual work its destination. Everything that follows in your Hoodoo practice flows from this moment of focused will.

Developing Mental Clarity

You already know you'll get distracted. The phone will buzz, thoughts will drift to tomorrow's worries, and focus will slip like water through your fingers. Don't expect spiritual work to magically bypass this reality.

Mental clarity isn't a gift granted by perfect conditions—it's a muscle you strengthen through consistent, unglamorous practice. Every time you notice your mind wandering during a working and deliberately pull it back to your candle, your intention, your breath, you're building the capacity your magic requires. Our ancestors didn't wait for quiet minds before working protection spells in the chaos of survival; they trained their focus until it became reliable under pressure.

Start with something embarrassingly simple: light a white candle and watch the flame for three minutes without letting your gaze wander. When your attention drifts—and it will—return to the flame without judgment. You're not failing; you're practicing the exact skill that separates scattered energy from directed force. Do this daily until three minutes feels easy, then extend to five.

Breath offers another anchor that costs nothing and travels with you everywhere. Before any working, place both feet flat on the floor and take three deliberate breaths—in through your nose for a count of four, out through your mouth for six. This isn't spiritual theater; it's physiology. Controlled breathing shifts your nervous system from scattered reactivity to focused presence. Research published in *Frontiers in Psychology* (Ma et al., 2017) shows that slow-paced breathing activates the parasympathetic nervous system, promoting calm and improved focus—creating the internal steadiness your magic needs to land with precision (Ma et al., 2017).

When intrusive thoughts arrive mid-working—"Did I lock the door?" or "What if this doesn't work?"—acknowledge them like passing clouds rather than storms requiring immediate attention. Name the thought silently: "worrying about doors" or "doubting," then return to your work. Each return strengthens your mental discipline more than an hour of unbroken concentration ever could, because you're training the exact redirect your practice will demand when stakes are highest.

Progress looks like noticing distractions faster, not eliminating them entirely.

Harnessing Emotional Resonance

Focused attention creates the channel, but **emotion supplies the current that moves through it**. A perfectly worded intention delivered without feeling arrives like a letter with no stamp—technically complete but going nowhere.

Your ancestors understood this instinctively. Across diverse cultures, from ancient rites to modern traditional practices, individuals infuse rituals with potent emotions—deep reverence, empathetic connection, or assertive intent. This emotional intensity is not a distraction; it is the core power, believed by practitioners to influence outcomes and connect with unseen forces (Whitehouse & Mc Kay, 2014). Emotions like anger at injustice, desperation for safety, or joy at new beginnings are not obstacles but potent fuel to be harnessed.

The mistake isn't feeling too much. It's feeling without direction.

Scattered emotion scatters results. Fear mixed with hope mixed with doubt creates contradictory signals that cancel each other out, leaving your working confused about what you're actually asking for. But when you identify the specific emotion your goal genuinely evokes—**prosperity work charged with grateful anticipation, protection spells powered by calm certainty, love work infused with openhearted courage**—you create coherent energy that spirits and natural forces can clearly receive and amplify.

This alignment between what you want and what you feel transforms mechanical ritual into living magic. When emotional resonance matches stated intention, the working gains exponential force. You're no longer performing magic; you're *embodying* it, which is precisely what moves mountains and shifts circumstances that seemed immovable.

Chapter Five

Essential Materials and Tools: Herbs, Roots, Minerals, and Symbolic Objects

Herbs and Roots: Nature's Toolbox for Magic

Identifying Magical Herbs

hen your grandmother crushed basil leaves into her hands before a difficult conversation, she wasn't making potpourri. She was activating protection. When the root worker three counties over sent you a small brown root wrapped in red flannel with instructions to keep it close, that wasn't theater. That was **High John the Conqueror**, and it held generations of documented power.

Most beginners approach herbs like they're shopping for candles—choosing by color, by what sounds pretty, by what some online list promised would solve everything. That approach wastes your money and dilutes your work. **Hoodoo herbs aren't interchangeable.** Each one carries specific energies shaped by centuries of use, each one speaks to particular needs, and each one demands you know exactly what you're holding.

Recognition is power. You need to identify your materials by sight, scent, and touch—not just by the label someone else printed. Dried basil leaves look nothing like crushed angelica root. *Can you tell the difference when both are powdered?* That knowledge separates working magic from wishful thinking.

Start with the essentials used across generations: basil for protection and clearing paths, High John root for strength and overcoming obstacles, and graveyard dirt for ancestral connection. Learn how each looks fresh versus dried, how it smells when crushed, what texture it carries in your palm. This tactile knowledge builds authenticity into every working you perform, ensuring that when you reach for an herb in the middle of a spell, you're holding exactly what your intention requires.

Sourcing and Ethical Gathering

The most common misconception beginners bring to sourcing Hoodoo materials is that **authentic means expensive** or requires special access to hidden suppliers. You don't need to spend hundreds on rare imports when the root worker two generations back gathered most materials within walking distance of her back door.

Ethical sourcing in this practice means two things: respecting the earth that provides and respecting the cultural context that shaped these traditions. When you strip bark from a living tree without permission or gratitude, you're not practicing Hoodoo—you're practicing theft. When you harvest an entire patch of wild roots because you can, leaving nothing for regeneration, you've broken the reciprocity that makes this work function.

Most practitioners build their collections through three paths. You purchase dried herbs from reputable suppliers who can verify botanical identity—because receiving oregano when you ordered hyssop isn't just inconvenient, it fundamentally changes your working. You grow your own when possible, establishing direct relationship with the plants from seed to harvest. You wildcraft selectively, gathering from nature with permission, never taking more than a third of what you find, and offering something in return—a coin, tobacco, your gratitude spoken aloud.

Wildcrafting requires genuine knowledge. Misidentifying plants can poison your work or poison you. If you cannot distinguish Solomon's Seal from similar-looking toxic species, such as Lily of the Valley, you have no business digging roots in the woods (Tyrant Farms, 2022). This isn't gatekeeping—it's survival.

Building a personal collection means starting small with verified essentials rather than hoarding dozens of half-understood materials. Five herbs you know intimately outperform fifty you've never touched. Buy whole forms when possible—whole leaves over powder, whole roots over chips—because you need to see what you're working with.

Sustainability isn't optional or modern sensitivity. Your ancestors understood that depleting resources meant losing access to power. That principle hasn't changed because you're shopping online instead of walking creek beds.

Applications in Rituals

Herbs hold their power not just in their nature, but in how you work with them. You can steep them into teas that carry your intentions with every sip, bundle them into sachets that radiate energy wherever they rest, or dissolve them into baths that cleanse and transform from skin to spirit. Each method channels the plant's essence differently, and understanding these pathways lets you choose the most potent form for your specific working.

Teas and infusions draw out the water-soluble properties of herbs, creating drinkable magic that enters your body directly. When you craft a tea for courage, clarity, or attraction, you're not just consuming herbs—you're inviting their qualities to merge with your own energy. Boil water, pour it over your chosen herbs, let them steep while you speak your intention, then strain and drink slowly, feeling each sip align you with your purpose. This method works beautifully for internal shifts: calming anxiety, enhancing intuition, or drawing love toward you.

Sachets and mojo bags contain herbs in small fabric pouches that you carry, hide, or place strategically. Fill a small cloth square with your chosen herbs, add any roots or personal concerns, tie it closed while stating your intention, and carry it in your pocket or purse. For protection, tuck it above your doorway. For prosperity, keep it near your wallet. The herbs release their energy slowly and steadily, creating a constant field of influence around the object or person they accompany.

Spiritual baths immerse your entire body in herbal water, washing away what no longer serves while drawing in what you need. Steep your herbs in hot water as you would for tea, strain the plant material, add the liquid to your bathwater along with any oils or salts, then step in and soak. As you bathe, visualize the water pulling negativity down the drain while the herbs' properties soak into your skin. This method excels at clearing, protection, and attraction work—anything that needs to touch you completely.

You can also **burn herbs as incense**, releasing their smoke to cleanse spaces or carry prayers upward, or **dress candles** by crushing dried herbs and rolling anointed candles through them. Some practitioners create **floor washes** by steeping herbs and using the strained liquid to mop doorways and thresholds, literally washing intentions into the foundation of their home.

Choose your method based on what feels right for your working. Internal change? Tea. Portable protection? Sachet. Deep cleansing? Bath. Trust your instincts—they know which pathway will carry your intention most powerfully into manifestation.

Symbolism and Energetic Properties

When rootworkers speak of herbs carrying specific energies, they're not speaking poetically—they're describing measurable effects that show up consistently across generations of practice. **Basil draws money** not because someone decided it should, but because practitioners noticed again and again that carrying basil leaves shifted financial circumstances (Art of the Root, 2015; This Crooked Crown, 2015; Revolutionary Mystic, 2024; Still Jacey, 2025). **Rue repels negativity** because people who planted it by their doors stopped experiencing the strange illnesses and bad luck that plagued them before (aromaG's Botanica, n.d.; Original Botanica, 2023; Smudge Metaphysical Spiritual Boutique, n.d.; Vickygardens, n.d.; Wax Spiritual, n.d.; Wax Spiritual, 2024). This isn't faith. It's accumulated evidence.

These patterns emerged from necessity. Enslaved practitioners couldn't afford superstition—their survival depended on knowing which plants actually worked (Pub Med, 1987; Original Botanica, 2025; Llewellyn, 2003; Llewellyn, 2004; Ginseng, Hoodoo, and the Magic of Upholding African American Earth-Based Traditions, 2021; Medium, 2026; Wikipedia, n.d.; Medium, 2024). When a grandmother told you to wear High John root for strength, she wasn't sharing folklore. She was passing down knowledge tested through hardship, refined through desperation, proven through results that meant the difference between enduring and breaking.

Each herb carries what we call its **spiritual signature**—the energetic quality that makes it useful for specific work (The Power of High John the Conqueror Root in Hoodoo, 2025; World-Of-Conjure, 2024; Scribd, n.d.; Matthew Wood Institute of Herbalism, 2023). Lavender calms because its essence naturally soothes turbulent energy. Cinnamon heats up situations because its fiery nature accelerates movement and change. Understanding these signatures means you're not just following recipes. You're learning to read the language plants speak, recognizing which energies your intention needs to manifest in the physical world.

This knowledge transforms how you work. Instead of wondering whether your spell will function, you choose herbs whose proven properties align with your goal. You combine them deliberately, layering their energies to create exactly the spiritual condition your intention requires. That's when magic stops feeling like wishful thinking and starts feeling like the practical tool it's always been.

• • •

Minerals and Elements: Harnessing Earth's Power

Identifying Essential Minerals

Minerals carry a different kind of power than herbs. They don't dry out or lose potency. They don't need sunlight or water. They simply *are*—unchanged for thousands of years, holding earth's memory in physical form.

Salt stands as the foundation mineral in Hoodoo work, and your ancestors understood why. It purifies, protects, and creates impenetrable barriers against negative energy. Not because someone declared it magical, but because enslaved practitioners noticed that evil seemed unable to cross salt lines, that homes protected with salt experienced fewer spiritual disturbances. You'll use it constantly: sprinkled across thresholds to block unwanted influences, dissolved in baths to strip away attachments, mixed into floor washes to cleanse spaces. Sea salt carries ocean's vast clearing power; kosher salt works for everyday protection. The white granules you see are compressed minerals formed under immense pressure—that density makes them spiritually dense, too heavy for negative energy to penetrate.

Iron protects through strength rather than purity. Railroad spikes, horseshoes, nails—these weren't chosen randomly. Iron's magnetic properties disrupt harmful spiritual forces the way magnets scramble electronic signals. Rootworkers buried railroad spikes at property corners because they observed that homes so protected experienced fewer curses and intrusions. Place iron under your bed for nightmare protection, hang horseshoes above doorways, carry a small nail for personal defense.

Lodestone functions differently—it attracts rather than repels. These naturally magnetic rocks physically pull iron filings toward themselves, and that drawing power extends spiritually. Feed your lodestone with magnetic sand, whisper what you need, and it pulls those energies toward you with the same inexorable force that makes metal move.

Each mineral offers what roots cannot: permanence, density, and elemental force unchanged since earth's formation.

Sourcing and Preparing Minerals

Ethical sourcing begins with knowing who to trust. Reputable metaphysical shops, often run by practitioners themselves, sell properly identified minerals at fair prices and provide clear information about origin. They don't rename common materials to justify inflated costs. Online suppliers like **Lucky Mojo Curio Company** and **Carolina Conjure** have earned their standing within the practitioner community through accuracy and integrity.

Watch for red flags. Any shop selling "authentic graveyard dirt" harvested without permission lacks respect for the practice. Lodestones priced absurdly high when natural magnetite costs far less signal exploitation. Suppliers who cannot or will not disclose where their materials come from should be avoided entirely.

Most basic materials don't require specialty suppliers at all. Salt comes from the grocery store, iron nails from the hardware store, and lodestones—really just magnetite—from rock shops. Discernment matters more than exclusivity.

When wildcrafting or collecting iron objects yourself, remember the principle of exchange. Earth gives generously, but she remembers theft. Always offer something in return: tobacco, coins, a prayer. This isn't superstition; it's ancestral understanding made practical.

Before any mineral touches your work, cleanse it. Minerals absorb energy like sponges, picking up everything they encounter. Clearing those accumulated energies is essential.

Running water works for most minerals. Hold them under a stream for several minutes, visualizing previous energies washing away. Natural flowing water offers stronger clearing power, but tap water functions just fine. **Smoke cleansing** purifies minerals that water might damage—pass them through frankincense, sage, or cedar smoke, typically seven passes minimum, until you feel the shift. **Burial** allows earth to reclaim and neutralize energy completely. Bury minerals in clean soil for three days, marking the spot so you can find them again.

Once cleansed, **consecration** dedicates the mineral to your specific purpose. Hold the material and state your intention clearly: "This salt protects my threshold from all harm." Breathe onto it three times. Some practitioners anoint minerals with condition oils matching their purpose—Protection Oil for iron, Money-Drawing Oil for lodestone. This consecration bonds your will to the mineral's natural properties, creating a tool calibrated precisely to your need rather than one carrying only generic potential.

Harnessing Elemental Energies

Salt carries the cleansing power of water and earth combined, making it one of the most versatile protectors in your Hoodoo toolkit. When you sprinkle salt across your doorway, you're not just scattering white crystals—you're invoking **ancient elemental forces** that purify and shield. Iron connects deeply with fire's transformative energy and earth's grounding strength, creating barriers that spiritual harm cannot cross. Lodestone pulses with magnetic earth energy, drawing what you desire toward you with an almost irresistible pull.

Each mineral resonates with specific elemental frequencies that amplify your intentions when you understand how to work with them.

Fire minerals like iron and sulfur ignite action and transformation in your spells. **Water-aligned minerals** such as salt and sea minerals cleanse, purify, and flow around obstacles blocking your path. **Earth minerals** including lodestone, graveyard dirt, and pyrite ground your work in tangible reality, manifesting results you can see and touch.

Air-associated minerals like crystal quartz carry your prayers upward and clarify muddled situations.

Start simply. Place a small dish of salt in each corner of a room while visualizing water washing away stagnant energy and earth absorbing negativity into itself.

Feel the shift as the space lightens.

For a protection ritual using iron's fierce energy, position iron nails at entry points to your home, speaking aloud your intention that no harmful force may enter. The iron anchors your command in both the fire element's protective rage and earth's immovable strength. When working with lodestone to draw prosperity, hold the stone between your palms and visualize earth's magnetic pull gathering opportunities, money, and success toward you like iron filings. Feed your lodestone regularly with magnetic sand, sustaining its **elemental connection** and keeping its drawing power strong.

These aren't abstract concepts—they're practical techniques that connect your spiritual work directly to the **living forces** running through creation itself.

• • •

Symbolic Objects and Personal Concerns: Creating a Personal Connection

The Power of Personal Connection in Hoodoo

Personal concerns are items carrying someone's physical essence—hair, fingernails, signature, worn clothing, photographs. They create spiritual links to specific individuals, functioning as direct pathways that bypass generalized energy work entirely. When you hold a strand of someone's hair while speaking intention, you're not symbolically connecting to them; you're working with their actual cellular material, which traditional practitioners understood carry spiritual imprint.

Collect personal concerns ethically. Never take these items without permission unless working justified protection against genuine harm. Your own concerns prove most accessible and powerful for self-work: trim your hair during a waxing moon for growth spells, use nail clippings in prosperity sachets, sign your name on petition papers to anchor your will. Save strands from your brush, keep photographs that capture you in moments of strength, preserve fabric swatches from clothing worn during significant achievements.

Symbolic objects work differently—they represent intentions through recognized correspondences that spirits and natural forces understand.

Keys unlock opportunities when charged with opening energy and carried during job searches. Lodestones attract desired outcomes through magnetic resonance when fed regularly with magnetic sand. Coins multiply prosperity through their literal exchange value when dressed with money-drawing oil and placed in cash registers. Each object speaks a language the spiritual realm comprehends without translation.

Start simple: choose one symbolic object aligned with your immediate need. Hold it between your palms, speak your intention three times with absolute clarity, breathe onto it to transfer your will. Carry it daily, touching it whenever doubt surfaces. Feed living symbols like lodestones weekly; refresh static objects monthly by repeating your charge. This builds relationship between your energy and the object's inherent properties, transforming ordinary items into potent spiritual allies.

Gathering and Preparing Symbolic Materials Ethically

Progress comes through doing, not waiting for perfect clarity. You won't feel entirely ready the first time you gather hair from your brush for protection work or select a coin for prosperity. Your hands might hesitate when cleansing a newly acquired lodestone, uncertain if you're doing it correctly. Most beginners expect some mystical confirmation that they've prepared materials properly—a tingle, a vision, a sudden knowing.

Rarely happens that way.

What actually builds competence is repeating the process until your hands move with confidence. Cleanse that second lodestone more smoothly than the first. Speak intentions over symbolic objects without stumbling through words you've practiced three times already. Collect your own hair clippings on the waxing moon, store them properly labeled in a clean jar, and use them when needed rather than scrambling during crisis.

Common obstacles will surface. You'll forget to cleanse something and wonder if the work is compromised. You'll realize halfway through a spell that you grabbed the wrong symbolic object. You'll misplace that photograph you intended to use and feel like the universe is blocking your progress. None of these derail your practice permanently.

Cleanse the item now if you forgot earlier—better late than never, and intention carries real weight. Use a different symbolic object if the first choice isn't available; coins work for prosperity whether they're the specific ones you planned to use or different ones charged with clear purpose. Substitute another photograph or skip it entirely if the spell works without it.

Hoodoo survived centuries of slavery and displacement precisely because practitioners adapted to limitations without abandoning their power (Chireau, 2006). Your first petition paper will probably have crossed-out words or uneven writing. Your initial attempts at feeding lodestones might feel awkward, like you're performing rather than practicing. These imperfections don't invalidate the work. **Ancestors didn't have pristine conditions or unlimited materials—they worked with what survived the Middle Passage, what grew in hostile soil, what they could hide from those who would destroy their traditions.**

Start where you are. Gather one personal concern this week. Select one symbolic object that resonates with your most pressing need. Cleanse it, charge it, work with it. Notice what shifts—not dramatic transformations, but subtle movements toward your intention. Then do it again, building confidence through repetition rather than waiting for certainty that never arrives before action.

Activating and Using Personal Concerns in Spellwork

Bringing personal concerns and symbolic objects together transforms isolated materials into living spiritual work. You've learned that hair or fingernails carry your unique signature, that lodestones pull toward you magnetically, that mirrors deflect harm, that coins resonate with prosperity (Yronwode, 2002). **The real shift happens when you combine these elements deliberately**, creating spiritual constructs that address your actual needs rather than abstract possibilities.

Dress a photograph with attraction oil by dabbing it at the four corners while stating exactly what you want this person to feel toward you. Place it face-down over a lodestone you've already fed with magnetic sand. Speak your intention aloud three times, then position the whole assembly under a pink candle dressed with the same oil. Burn the candle in three-hour increments over three days, a method consistent with attraction work in Hoodoo. This simple working demonstrates how layering materials—photograph, lodestone, oil, candle—creates escalating spiritual pressure focused on a single clear outcome.

For protection, take a small mirror and your personal concern—hair works well. Glue the hair to the non-reflective side of the mirror while commanding it to turn back any harm sent your way. Wrap the mirror in red flannel with protective herbs like devil's shoestring and High John root. Carry it or hide it where you need defense most.

Name papers demonstrate directional power through simple technique: write the person's name (or your own) an odd number of times, rotate the paper ninety degrees, then write your intention crossing those names. Fold toward you to draw something closer, away from you to push something back. Each fold carries spoken intention. Place the folded paper under candles, inside mojo bags with complementary roots, or buried at specific locations depending on your goal.

A prosperity working might combine three silver coins with a name paper stating financial increase. Dress each coin with money-drawing oil, place them on the name paper folded toward you, add magnetic sand and Irish moss. Wrap everything in green cloth, tie with green thread while stating your need, then keep it where you handle money daily. Feed it weekly with whiskey and more oil.

When you finish working, some items get buried to continue their work underground. Others get hidden in private spaces—under mattresses, inside pillowcases, behind pictures. Candle remains go to crossroads or running water. **Disposal matters as much as creation** because spiritual work doesn't simply stop; it requires proper closure, as detailed in various Hoodoo traditions.

Chapter Six

Working with Personal Concerns: Building Spiritual Connections to Your Intentions

Understanding Personal Concerns: The Essence of Sympathetic Magic

Defining Personal Concerns

Every effective Hoodoo working includes a physical piece of the target individual. Hair from a lover's pillow, fingernail clippings, or a shirt worn for days carry the living essence of that person. These items are not mere symbols—they function as direct spiritual conduits, creating an unbreakable link between your intention and its recipient.

Personal concerns serve as spiritual addresses in the unseen world. When you fold someone's hair into a honey jar or bury their photograph at a crossroads, you are working directly on *them*, not an abstraction. A strand of hair, a drop of blood, or even handwriting retains their unique spiritual signature, maintaining connection to its source long after separation from the body. This is the heart of sympathetic magic—the understanding that part contains whole, that the fragment remembers the source.

African spiritual traditions, the deepest roots of Hoodoo, have always recognized physical matter and spiritual energy as inseparable. Hair fallen from the head, saliva on a cigarette butt, or clothing saturated with someone's sweat all carry what practitioners call **personal essence**—the irreducible spiritual fingerprint that makes magic precise and powerful. When you work with these materials, you bypass distance, time, and circumstance, reaching directly into the spiritual fabric that connects all things.

The Power of Sympathetic Magic

Sympathetic magic operates on a principle older than written language: like attracts like, and what was once connected remains connected (Original Botanica, 2024; My Cousins Coven, 2025). This is not philosophy—it is the operational law governing how personal concerns function in Hoodoo work.

When you burn a red candle dressed with cinnamon oil while speaking your lover's name, you invoke the first principle. Red resembles passion, cinnamon's heat mirrors desire, and the flame's upward movement pulls energy toward manifestation. These correspondences work because spiritual forces recognize symbolic language, responding to resonance between material and intention. This is *similarity magic*—using objects that resemble your goal to draw that reality closer (Original Botanica, 2024).

But personal concerns operate through the second, more potent principle: **contagion**. (Original Botanica, 2024; My Cousins Coven, 2025)

A photograph of your target creates similarity—it looks like them. Their actual hair, however, *was them*, grown from their body, saturated with their unique cellular signature. The spiritual connection doesn't break when hair falls or a nail gets clipped. Matter remembers its origin (Crescent City Conjure, 2018; Black Witch Coven, 2015). This explains why experienced practitioners prize bodily fluids, worn clothing, and handwriting above generic photographs or name papers (Association of Independent

Readers and Rootworkers, 2025; Black Witch Coven, 2015; Personal Concerns, n.d.). Tears carry an emotional imprint. Sweat holds the body's salt and effort. Blood is the ultimate personal concern, containing the entirety of someone's physical blueprint (Crescent City Conjure, 2018; Black Witch Coven, 2015; Personal Concerns, n.d.).

Each substance maintains its sympathetic link, functioning as a living wire between your working and its intended recipient, regardless of physical distance. You can work justice on someone across the country if you have their signature. You can draw love from someone you haven't seen in years if you kept their shirt. The connection persists because spiritual law recognizes no separation between part and whole—only continuation of essence through different forms.

This is why Hoodoo demands physical components rather than abstract visualization alone.

Ethical Gathering and Usage

This power demands responsibility that most beginners never consider.

Working with someone's hair, photograph, or signature without their knowledge creates a spiritual connection they didn't consent to, binding your intention to their essence whether they agree or not. Some practitioners dismiss this concern, arguing that Hoodoo developed under conditions where enslaved people had no power except what they could claim covertly—utilizing spiritual practices for survival and resistance against oppressors. That historical context is real and deserves honoring. But it doesn't answer the ethical question standing before you now: just because you *can* work on someone without permission doesn't mean you **should**.

Your ancestors used these methods to survive impossible circumstances. You likely face different stakes.

Consider what you're actually doing when you take someone's personal concern without consent. You're deciding you know better than they do what should happen in their life. You're overriding their spiritual autonomy because your desired outcome matters more than their right to choose. This creates karmic debt—not because some cosmic accountant keeps score, but because **reciprocity is fundamental** to spiritual work. What you send out returns, amplified.

Some situations genuinely require covert work. Protection from an abuser who would escalate if they knew you were taking spiritual action. Justice work against someone causing active harm. These exist in the tradition for good reason, rooted in Hoodoo's historical use for protection and justice during times of extreme vulnerability. But drawing love from someone who rejected you? Controlling a boss who annoyed you? These aren't survival—they're spiritual overreach dressed as necessity.

The clearest guideline: **obtain consent whenever possible**.

Ask before taking hair from a brush. Explain why you want that photograph. Many people will agree if your intention benefits them. When consent isn't possible, examine your true motivation with ruthless honesty. Fear or genuine protection? Desire or manipulation? The spirits know the difference, even when you're still lying to yourself.

· · ·

Ethical Gathering and Use of Personal Items: Respect and Responsibility

Principles of Respectful Collection

Consent isn't a soft suggestion in Hoodoo—it's spiritual law encoded in the tradition's DNA. When practitioners operated under enslavement, they worked without permission because survival demanded it. Their descendants carried that knowledge forward, but the ethical framework evolved alongside changed circumstances. You're not fleeing an overseer or protecting your family from being sold. You're navigating modern relationships where power dynamics exist but rarely approach life-or-death stakes.

Gathering someone's **personal effects** without their knowledge fundamentally means deciding your will matters more than theirs. You're choosing to bind their essence to your intention, creating a spiritual connection they never agreed to enter. That decision carries weight regardless of how pure you believe your motives to be. The tradition recognizes this power—rootworkers understood that tampering with another person's spiritual essence without permission creates ripples that extend far beyond the immediate spell. These ripples don't just affect the target; they rebound onto the practitioner, tangling their own spiritual path with unearned burdens and unintended consequences.

So what does **ethical gathering** actually look like?

When working on yourself, you hold complete authority. Your hair from your brush, your fingernail clippings, your handwritten name on paper—these belong to you absolutely. Collect them with clear intention, store them properly, and use them to direct your own spiritual current toward your goals. This self-sovereignty forms the foundation of personal power in Hoodoo. Nobody can give you permission to work on yourself except you, and nobody can stop you either.

Working for others requires their **explicit consent**. Not hints. Not assumptions. Not deciding on their behalf that they "really need" your help. You ask directly: "May I work a blessing for you?" or "Can you give me something personal to use in a protection spell for your benefit?" Their answer determines whether you proceed. If they say yes, you explain what you need and why. If they hesitate or refuse, you respect that boundary completely. Their spiritual autonomy isn't negotiable, even when you believe you know what's best for them.

Photographs require particular care. A photo carries someone's image, their captured moment, their visible essence frozen in time. Using someone's photograph in your work without permission violates the same principle as using their hair or clothing. If you're working for them with consent, ask for a photo they willingly provide. If you're working on yourself—perhaps to remember an ancestor or honor a relationship—choose images where your connection to that person is already established and understood. The photograph becomes part of your story, not an intrusion into theirs.

What about those gray areas where traditional practice and modern ethics seem to clash? The answer lies in honest self-examination. Are you taking this action because the situation genuinely demands it, or because asking permission feels uncomfortable? Discomfort isn't sufficient justification. Fear for someone's immediate physical safety might be—but that's a threshold you cross knowing the spiritual cost, not casually or frequently. Most situations don't meet that standard, and pretending they do insults both the tradition and your own integrity.

Respecting these boundaries doesn't weaken your magic. It strengthens it. When you work with freely given items, the spiritual connection flows clean and unobstructed. The person's essence cooperates with your intention rather than resisting it. Their consent becomes part of the working itself, amplifying rather than diminishing your power. You're not just manipulating energy—you're **co-creating** with another person's willing participation, even if that participation is simply handing you a strand of hair and saying, "Yes, help me."

This is how Hoodoo survives and grows. Not by clinging to practices rooted in desperate circumstances, but by honoring the **core principles** those circumstances revealed: respect for spiritual sovereignty, recognition of personal power, and understanding that true magic works with the currents of consent, not against them.

Proper Use in Spellwork

A woman came to me three years ago with a photograph of her sister folded inside a small red cloth bag.

The sister had been withdrawing—missed calls, cancelled visits, silence where conversation used to flow. My visitor wanted to work a **Road Opener spell** to clear whatever obstacles stood between them, a practice recognized in Hoodoo for clearing blockages and creating new opportunities. She brought the photo, a piece of their mother's old tablecloth, and seven silver dimes. She also brought something else: her sister's permission, obtained through an honest phone call where she'd said, "I want to do some spiritual work to help us reconnect. Can I use that photo from your birthday?"

That consent transformed everything about the working.

The spell itself followed traditional Road Opener structure. I instructed her to anoint the photo's corners with **Van Van oil** while speaking her sister's full name three times. Van Van oil is a traditional Hoodoo formula used for clearing obstacles, protection, and empowering other spells. Then she wrote her intention on brown paper torn from a grocery bag: *"Clear roads open between [sister's name] and me."* She folded the paper toward herself three times, placed the photo face-up on top, and wrapped both in the tablecloth square. The seven dimes went into the bundle—silver for clarity, seven for spiritual completion—and she tied it all together with white cotton string, knotting it seven times while repeating her intention.

Each morning for seven days, she held the bundle over burning frankincense smoke and prayed in her own words. Not scripted appeals to distant saints, but direct conversation with the spirit of connection itself: what they'd been to each other, what she hoped they'd become again, gratitude for the relationship's foundation even when the present felt fractured.

On the seventh day, she buried the bundle at a **literal crossroads**—a place where two paths intersect, symbolizing choices and new directions. This act is a traditional method of disposing of spell remains in various magical traditions, believed to scatter energy or connect with spirits. She walked away without looking back, as tradition requires, leaving the working to do its task.

Her sister called two days later.

Not magically transformed, not suddenly available for weekly dinners, but willing to talk about the distance between them. They met for coffee. Conversations resumed gradually, unevenly, like reconnecting requires in the actual world.

What made this working effective beyond the technical components was simple: the sister's consent meant she'd already opened a door, however slightly. The spell worked *with* that opening rather than forcing entry where none existed. Her conscious agreement aligned with the spiritual current instead of creating resistance the magic had to overcome.

This is **ethical integration** in practice—not theoretical purity, but real work respecting real boundaries while achieving real results. The importance of consent in spiritual practices is a key ethical consideration in modern magical work, emphasizing respect for free will and autonomy. You gather materials with permission. You explain your intention honestly. You perform techniques the tradition has tested across generations. You release the outcome rather than clutching at control.

The sister's willingness to be included in the work became part of the work itself. That's not weakness. That's how power actually moves through the world when you're not forcing it into channels it was never meant to flow.

• • •

Incorporating Personal Concerns into Your Magic: Practical Techniques and Applications

Choosing the Right Personal Concerns

Start with yourself. Pull a single strand of hair from your own head and hold it between thumb and forefinger. That's the simplest personal concern you'll ever work with, and it carries your complete spiritual signature.

Selecting the right personal concern depends on your intention. For quick protection, hair or nail clippings are ideal—easily obtained and carrying your cellular essence. Clip nails over a white cloth during a waxing moon for creation work, or a waning moon for obstacle removal. Store them in a dated glass vial, labeled and kept safe.

Photographs serve varied purposes. A current self-photo suits attraction or road-opening work, while one depicting your most confident self amplifies success spells. For relationship matters, select a natural photo of both individuals, avoiding stiff or forced poses that might create artificial energy.

Written names gain power through repeated use and recognition. Your full legal name on brown paper connects to official matters like court cases or employment. A long-held nickname retains the energy from every time you responded to it, making it potent for personal transformation work.

Clothing absorbs energy differently than other concerns. The shirt from your job interview holds your determination; a scarf worn during hardship embodies resilience. Snip a small, unnoticeable square from a hem or seam to capture that specific emotional state and intention.

Precision is key: match the concern to your intention. For grounding work, use nail clippings taken while barefoot on earth. To amplify confidence, use hair brushed while affirming your worth. For financial stability, use a coin carried for months, warmed by your body and intentions.

Fresh concerns work stronger than old ones, but both have their place in the practitioner's craft.

Preparing Personal Concerns for Use

Before you use any personal concern in your work, it requires two essential steps: **cleansing and energizing**. Skip these, and you're working with contaminated material—energy that carries every worry, argument, or stray thought that's touched that item.

Cleansing removes accumulated energy. The simplest method uses smoke. Pass your concern through frankincense or white sage smoke three times, turning it clockwise. Watch the smoke curl around it, carrying away everything that doesn't serve your intention. For water-safe items like coins or certain stones, rinse under cold running water while visualizing murky residue flowing away, then pat dry with a clean white cloth.

Salt works differently but equally well. Bury the personal concern in a small bowl of sea salt or kosher salt for at least three hours, preferably overnight. The salt draws out negativity like a poultice draws poison from a wound. Afterward, dispose of that salt immediately—don't reuse it. That salt has done its work and now carries what you just removed.

Once cleansed, your personal concern sits neutral. **Now you energize it with your specific intention.** Hold it between your palms and speak your purpose aloud, clearly and without hesitation. "This connects me to prosperity" or "This links to protection for my home." Let your breath warm it. Let your intention seep into every fiber or pixel.

Some workers dress personal concerns with condition oils matched to their purpose: Van Van oil for clearing roads, Fast Luck for opportunity, Crown of Success for achievement. One drop is enough. Anoint while stating your intention, then wrap the item in red flannel or parchment paper until you're ready to incorporate it into your working.

Integrating Concerns into Rituals

When you need to embed personal concerns into your spellwork, the placement determines everything. A photograph tucked carelessly into a mojo bag carries different weight than one positioned deliberately beneath a candle, facing upward, while you speak your intention aloud.

Start with the simplest technique: name papers combined with personal concerns. Write your full name nine times on unlined paper, using black ink. Turn the paper ninety degrees. Write your intention across your name three times—"protection," "prosperity," or whatever you're calling in. Place a strand of your hair, a nail clipping, or a small photograph in the center of this paper. Fold it toward you three times if you're drawing something to you, away from you if you're sending something away. Each fold carries purpose.

Dressing the folded packet amplifies its power. Hold it between your palms, breathe your intention into it three times, then anoint each corner with an oil matched to your goal—Protection Oil for safety work, Money Drawing Oil for prosperity. The oil seals your breath and intention into the paper itself.

Mojo bags offer portable, ongoing magic. Select a small flannel bag in a color that matches your intention—red for love, green for money, white for protection. Add your dressed name paper, then layer in herbs and roots that support your goal. A lodestone draws what you want closer; magnetic sand feeds it. Three silver dimes attract prosperity; devil's shoestring protects. Tuck your personal concern deep in the center, surrounded by these supporting ingredients. Tie the bag with thread in the corresponding color, knotting your intention in with each wrap.

Feed your mojo bag weekly. A drop of matching oil, a sprinkle of whiskey, or even your breath keeps it alive and working.

For candle work, personal concerns anchor your petition. Carve your name into the candle, then dress it with oil, stroking from wick to base if you're drawing something in, base to wick if you're pushing something away. Place your photograph or written petition underneath the candle holder. As the candle burns, it pulls your intention through the personal concern, creating a direct spiritual channel. Never leave candles unattended—this isn't superstition, it's safety.

Enhancing Outcomes with Personalization

You won't master this in a week, and that's exactly as it should be. Real proficiency develops through seasons, not sessions—through repeated attempts that sometimes flicker and fail before they finally catch fire.

Start where you are, not where you think you should be. If gathering your own hair feels uncomfortable, begin with name papers alone. If carving candles seems intimidating, dress them with oil and speak your intention clearly. Every practitioner who now works complex multi-day rituals once fumbled with their first mojo bag, overstuffed it, tied crooked knots, forgot to feed it. They kept going anyway.

The most common obstacle isn't lack of skill—it's the paralysis of wanting perfect results immediately. You'll second-guess whether you folded the paper correctly, whether you used enough oil, whether your intention was specific enough. This doubt weakens your work more than any technical error ever could. Hoodoo survived because enslaved practitioners couldn't afford perfectionism; they worked with what they had, trusted their clarity of purpose, and adjusted based on results.

When a working doesn't produce immediate results, resist the urge to pile on additional spells. Many practitioners, desperate, perform multiple workings within days with differing intentions, creating contradictory signals. This scattered energy often yields nothing. Instead, pause. Ground yourself. Then perform one simple, focused working—perhaps with a dressed name paper and a green candle—to create a clearer energetic push toward your desired outcome.

Track what actually happens. Keep notes—which personal concerns you used, what happened afterward, how long results took to manifest. Patterns emerge through documentation, not wishful thinking. Your own experience becomes your most reliable teacher, building a personal practice that honors tradition while fitting your actual life, your actual needs, your actual spiritual path.

Chapter Seven

Protection Magic: Step-by-Step Spells and Rituals for Home, Body, and Spirit

Guarding Your Home: Creating a Protective Sanctuary

Physical Barriers and Symbols

Your home carries more than furniture and memories. It holds energy—the residue of emotions, encounters, and intentions that seep into walls, settle into corners, and linger at thresholds. When something feels off—a persistent chill, sudden arguments erupting from nowhere, or a streak of misfortune that defies explanation—your space may be telling you it needs protection. These aren't coincidences. They're signals that uninvited energies have found their way in, and it's time to fortify your sanctuary.

Physical barriers in Hoodoo aren't symbolic gestures; they're active shields. Salt laid across doorways stops harmful spirits from entering. Protective herbs tucked into window frames create energetic boundaries. Sigils drawn with intention transform ordinary entrances into guarded gates. Each element works through both its natural properties and the power you invest in it, creating layers of defense that negative forces cannot easily penetrate.

Start with **salt**—simple, potent, purifying. Sprinkle a thin line across every threshold: front door, back door, windows you open regularly. As you lay it down, speak your intention aloud. "This home is sealed. Only good may enter here." Salt absorbs negativity and creates an energetic barrier that repels malicious intent. Refresh it weekly, or immediately after sensing disturbance.

Next, work with **protective herbs**. Basil guards against evil. Rue breaks curses and sends harm back to its source. Angelica root calls on ancestral protection. Bundle these herbs in small cloth sachets and place them at entry points—above doors, tucked into window sills, hidden near corners where energy tends to stagnate. These aren't decorations; they're sentinels standing watch while you sleep.

Sigils amplify your defenses. Draw protective symbols—a simple X, a circle with a dot at center, or traditional Hoodoo markings—on doorframes using blessed oil or even your own saliva mixed with salt. These marks are invisible to casual eyes but unmistakable to spiritual forces. They declare: this space is claimed, protected, and not available for trespass.

Your home becomes a sanctuary not through hope, but through deliberate action. Guard it fiercely.

Rituals for Spiritual Protection

Once your physical barriers stand ready, the deeper work begins. Spiritual guardians don't arrive because you've lit a candle and wished. They respond to invitation, respect, and clear understanding of what you're asking. **Invoking protective spirits requires knowing who you're calling and why they would answer.**

Ancestors stand first among your spiritual defenders. They've walked this earth, understand its dangers, and maintain interest in their bloodline's welfare. To invite their protection, create a simple ancestor altar—a white cloth, a glass of water, their photographs if you have them, and a white candle. Speak to them directly: "Grandmothers and grandfathers of my blood, I ask you to stand watch over this home. Guard us against harm seen and unseen." Light the candle on Monday evenings, refresh the water weekly, and listen for their guidance in dreams and sudden knowing.

Timing matters. Protection work gains strength during the waning moon, when energy naturally turns toward banishing and boundaries. Midnight, the witching hour, holds particular power for sealing spaces against malevolent forces. Dawn works equally well—the moment when darkness retreats and new light claims the world.

Your materials should include blessed salt, protective oil (olive oil infused with basil, rue, and angelica), and frankincense or sage for cleansing smoke. Basil, rue, and angelica are all herbs traditionally associated with protection. Begin at your front door, moving clockwise through each room. Anoint doorframes with oil while speaking aloud: "By oil and intention, this threshold is sealed."

When you sense resistance—a room that feels heavy, a corner that holds shadow even in daylight—that's where concentrated work is needed. Stand in that space, burn your cleansing herb, and command firmly: "What does not serve this household must leave. You have no power here." *Do not ask.* Do not negotiate. Claim your authority.

The work concludes when the space feels lighter, when you can breathe fully in every room without inexplicable tightness in your chest.

Protective Talismans and Charms

Spiritual guardians alone won't secure your home. Physical objects, properly prepared and placed, create tangible barriers that hold energy long after your attention moves elsewhere. **A protective charm is spiritual intention made solid**—something you can touch, position strategically, and renew when necessary.

Materials matter because they already carry inherent properties. *Red flannel* naturally holds protective energy, which is why it appears in traditional mojo bags across generations. Iron nails driven into earth repel malevolent spirits and wandering shadows alike, a practice rooted in European folk magic. Salt crystallizes boundaries, a common protective element in many cultures. Black tourmaline absorbs negative energy without releasing it back into your space, according to crystal healing traditions. Choose materials that resonate with your intention, and the charm will hold stronger. (Tyson, 2018)

To create a basic protection charm, cut a square of red flannel approximately four inches across. Place inside it three ingredients chosen for specific purpose: **angelica root** for guardian spirit presence, **black salt** for absorbing harmful intentions, and a **rusty iron nail** for physical defense. As you add each item, state its function aloud—not as request but as declaration. "This angelica calls protection. This salt devours malice. This iron repels all harm." (Cunningham, 1985)

Draw the corners together and bind them with black thread, winding it nine times while visualizing your home surrounded by impenetrable walls of light. Knot it three times.

The activation matters as much as the construction. Hold the finished charm in both hands and breathe into it—your actual breath, carrying your intention. Speak: "You are awake. You stand guard. Nothing crosses this threshold without my permission." The charm now holds not just ingredients but living purpose.

Position these at cardinal points of your home—north, south, east, west—or bury them at the four corners of your property if you have land. Place one above your front door, another beneath your bed.

Charms don't last forever. When one feels lighter in your hand, when its fabric frays, or when you sense its potency fading, it's done its work. Bury it with thanks and create a fresh one. This isn't failure—it's completion.

Daily Maintenance Practices

Protection isn't a single act. It's a rhythm you establish, habits so small they slip into your mornings and evenings without feeling like extra work. **Daily reinforcement builds cumulative power**—each repetition strengthens what you've already set in place.

Start with threshold checks. Every morning before you leave, run your hand along your front doorframe. Feel for temperature shifts, unexpected stickiness, or spots that make your palm tingle. These subtle changes signal energy attempting entry. When you notice them, reapply your protective powders or oils immediately.

Sweeping matters more than you think. Physical dirt carries spiritual residue—tracked-in negativity, lingering arguments, stagnant frustration from difficult days. **Sweep toward your back door at least three times weekly**, pushing everything out and away from your living space. As you sweep, maintain clear intention: "All that doesn't serve leaves now." The motion itself becomes ritual.

Monday mornings, light a white candle and walk your home's perimeter, even if it's just a small apartment. You're not performing elaborate ceremony—you're checking your spiritual fence line. Notice where energy feels heavy or rooms that suddenly seem darker despite adequate lighting. These spots need immediate attention through smoke cleansing or salt placement.

Keep a small dish of salt water on your kitchen counter, changed every three days. Salt absorbs what enters your home through conversation, visitors, and your own emotional states. When the water clouds or develops sediment faster than usual, something's working harder to get in.

The most overlooked practice: *intentional silence.* Once weekly, sit in your home's center for five minutes without distraction. Listen to how your space sounds, feels, breathes. You'll recognize when something shifts—when energy changes texture or unfamiliar presences attempt residence. This quiet monitoring catches vulnerabilities before they become problems, giving you time to reinforce weak points before genuine threats establish themselves.

Habits seem minor until you miss them and notice the difference.

• • •

Shielding Your Body: Personal Protection Spells and Rituals

Crafting Protective Amulets

Personal protective amulets create a shield that moves with you beyond the sanctuary of your home. The work differs from stationary protections—these objects rest against your skin, breathe with you, and absorb impacts intended for your spirit.

Selection matters more than you might think. Red flannel bags remain the traditional choice because red repels malevolent energy while flannel holds scent and intention. Black flannel shields against specific curses. Leather pouches work for those who sweat heavily or live in humid climates. Glass bottles sealed with wax provide permanent protection but lack flexibility. Choose what you'll actually wear consistently, tucked beneath clothing or carried in a left pocket near your heart.

The filling creates the actual barrier. High John the Conqueror root establishes dominance over hostile forces. Angelica root draws guardian spirits close. Devil's shoestring tangles ill intent directed toward you. **Black salt**—salt mixed with ash or iron oxide—absorbs negativity like a sponge. A pinch of sulfur repels unwanted attention. Three iron nails create an impenetrable spiritual fence. You don't need everything; select three to five ingredients that address your specific vulnerability.

Assemble your amulet during the waning moon when protective work gains strength. Sit in silence, grounding yourself through breath until your hands feel warm. Hold each ingredient separately, stating its purpose aloud: "Angelica root, you draw my ancestors near to shield me." This isn't metaphor—you're waking the material's inherent properties and aligning them with your need. Place items into your vessel one at a time, building layers of defense.

Your breath activates everything. Once filled, hold the closed amulet between both palms. Breathe onto it three times, each exhalation carrying clear intention: "You are my shield. No harm touches me. I walk protected." The warmth from your hands, moisture from your breath, and certainty in your voice transfer your personal energy into the object. This makes it specifically yours—attuned to your spiritual signature rather than generic.

Wear it immediately. The amulet strengthens through contact, absorbing your scent and body heat. When it feels lighter or incidents increase despite wearing it, the protection has depleted. Bury it at a crossroads with thanks, then create a fresh one.

Daily Protective Rituals

A woman in South Carolina came to me after weeks of escalating trouble—flat tires, sudden arguments with colleagues who'd always been cordial, a persistent cold that wouldn't break. She'd been carrying a protection bag for three months without incident until the attacks began. When I examined her amulet, it felt oddly light, almost hollow. The red flannel had faded to dusty pink.

Protection doesn't maintain itself. Materials absorb negativity directed at you, gradually filling like a cup under a slow drip. When saturated, they lose effectiveness—

sometimes catastrophically. She'd made one critical error: treating the amulet as a lucky charm rather than a working tool. No monthly check-ins, no recharging under moonlight, no attention to warning signs her body had been sending. The exhausted protection left her vulnerable to precisely what it should have deflected.

I taught her what experienced practitioners know instinctively.

Every Monday morning, hold your amulet in both hands and *feel* its weight. Fresh protection feels dense, almost warm. Depleted materials feel light, cool, slightly rough. Temperature matters—if it runs cold against your skin when it typically feels neutral, something's draining it faster than usual.

Recharge before depletion. Once monthly during the waxing moon, set your amulet on a white cloth sprinkled with salt. Light a white candle beside it. Speak directly: "I restore your strength. You continue protecting me." Leave it overnight, then wear it again at dawn. This simple ritual extends effectiveness considerably.

When recharging stops working—when the amulet feels persistently light or incidents continue despite monthly maintenance—replacement becomes necessary, not optional. She buried her exhausted protection at a crossroads before sunrise, thanking it for service rendered. The new amulet I helped her construct held strong for eight months before requiring its first recharge.

She learned to listen.

Emergency Protection Techniques

Sometimes danger doesn't announce itself. It arrives in a crowded room, a tense conversation, or the prickling sensation along your spine that tells you something isn't right. In these moments, you need protection that's **immediate, discreet, and powerful**—magic you can summon without drawing attention, without elaborate preparation, without second-guessing yourself.

These rapid-response techniques are your spiritual first aid kit. They work because they're rooted in the oldest Hoodoo principle: **intention channeled through focused action creates instant change**. When you're standing in a hostile environment or facing unexpected negativity, you don't have time to light candles or mix oils. You need protection that lives in your body, in your breath, in the gestures your hands can make while tucked inside your pockets. These techniques anchor quickly because they bypass complexity—they're pure intention meeting pure action, the way our ancestors protected themselves when they had nothing but their own spiritual power and their connection to the unseen.

The **breath shield** is your first line of defense. When you sense threat, take three slow, deliberate breaths, pulling protective energy up from the earth with each inhale. Visualize white or blue light filling your chest, expanding outward with each exhale to form an invisible barrier around your body. This takes fifteen seconds. No one watching will know you're building a wall they cannot penetrate, yet you'll feel the shift immediately—a subtle strengthening, a sense of being untouchable.

The **mirror gesture** works when words become weapons. As someone directs negativity toward you, discreetly cross your first two fingers or press your thumb against your ring finger inside your pocket. Silently affirm: *"Your words return to you; I reflect what is not mine."* This simple gesture redirects harmful energy back to its source without absorbing it yourself. It's particularly effective in arguments, manipulative conversations, or when you're the target of gossip or ill will.

For situations requiring stronger intervention, invoke the **ancestral call**. Speak silently or whisper the names of your protective ancestors or spiritual allies, asking them to stand between you and harm. Feel their presence gathering around you like an invisible wall of witnesses. This technique carries profound power because you're not facing danger alone—you're surrounded by those who've walked through fire before you and emerged whole.

Keep a **protection token** on your body always: a small piece of iron in your pocket, a silver coin, or a tiny pouch of salt sealed with red thread. When you need immediate shielding, grip it tightly while visualizing yourself surrounded by impenetrable light. This physical anchor helps focus your intention when your mind is racing, giving your protection work something solid to cling to.

Practice these techniques now, before you need them. The power of rapid-response protection lies not in their complexity but in their **instant availability**—they become reflexes, spiritual muscle memory that activates the moment danger appears.

• • •

Defending Your Spirit: Spiritual Fortification Techniques

Creating a Protective Aura

Protection begins within. Before you worry about crosses over doorways or salt lines across thresholds, you must first tend to the fortress of your own spirit. Your spiritual essence—your soul's light, your inner fire—requires deliberate fortification, especially when you navigate spaces thick with hostility, envy, or unseen malevolence.

Visualization is the foundation of spiritual defense. Each morning, before your feet touch the floor, close your eyes and envision a radiant sphere of white or golden light emanating from your center. See it expanding outward, forming a luminous shield that surrounds your entire body. This isn't mere imagination; you are commanding spiritual energy to arrange itself according to your will. Hold this image for at least thirty seconds, feeling the warmth and weight of this protective barrier settling around you like an invisible cloak.

Your intention gives this visualization its power.

Speak your protection into being. Whisper words such as, "I am shielded by divine light. No harm may penetrate my spirit. I walk in sacred protection." These affirmations aren't flowery declarations—they are **spiritual commands** that reinforce the energetic boundary you've just constructed. Repeat them daily, and they will become woven into the very fabric of your being.

To strengthen this practice, carry a small personal talisman—a silver dime, a smooth lodestone, or a snippet of High John the Conqueror root wrapped in red flannel. Hold it during your morning visualization, charging it with your protective intention. Throughout the day, when you sense negative energy pressing against your boundaries, touch this talisman and recall the image of your luminous shield. This physical anchor helps you instantly reconnect with your spiritual fortification, even in the midst of chaos.

Your spirit, when properly defended, becomes unshakeable—a sacred sanctuary that moves with you wherever you go.

Calling on Ancestral Guardians

You are not alone in this work. Before your breath, before your bones, generations of ancestors walked these same spiritual paths, navigating dangers you cannot yet imagine. They survived. They protected. They endured. And now, their strength remains available to you, waiting for your invitation.

Connecting with ancestral guardians doesn't require elaborate ceremony or psychic gifts. Start simply: create a small ancestor space in your home. A white cloth covers a shelf or table. Place a glass of fresh water, a white candle, and photographs of known ancestors if you have them. If you don't know their faces, that's fine—place meaningful objects that honor your lineage. A small bowl of rice or cornmeal acknowledges their sacrifice.

Speak to them directly, aloud. "Grandmothers and grandfathers, known and unknown, I ask you to stand with me. I need your protection. I need your wisdom. Guide my steps." This isn't begging—it's recognizing relationship. They have vested interest in your survival; your thriving honors their struggle. Say their names if you know them. Speak weekly, keeping the water fresh and the candle burning when you need their presence near.

When facing specific threats, intensify the connection.

Light the white candle and state your situation plainly: "There is hostility at my workplace. Someone wishes me harm. I ask my ancestors to shield me, to stand between me and this malice." Then listen. Protection often arrives as sudden insight, an inexplicable change in circumstances, or the feeling of invisible hands steadying you during crisis. Some weeks you'll feel nothing. That's normal. Keep showing up anyway, refreshing the water, lighting the candle, speaking your gratitude.

Ancestral protection builds gradually, like muscle or trust, strengthening through consistent acknowledgment rather than desperate pleas. You will stumble. You'll forget offerings or doubt whether any of this matters. Return anyway. Your ancestors understand human weakness—they possessed it too. What matters is continuation, the choice to keep reaching across the veil for the protection that has always been your birthright.

Rituals for Spiritual Armor

These rituals form your **spiritual armor**—not metaphorical protection, but actual barriers between your spirit and forces that would diminish it. Protective amulets worn against skin, breath shields deployed in seconds, ancestor altars tended with water and candlelight all serve this purpose.

Each technique addresses different vulnerabilities. The amulet creates mobile defense, absorbing impacts throughout your day. Rapid-response methods offer immediate intervention when a threat appears suddenly—hostile words, psychic aggression, environments thick with malevolent energy. Ancestral connection provides reinforcement that transcends your individual capacity, drawing on generations of accumulated spiritual strength. Together, they create layered fortification: physical materials charged with intention, trained reflexes activating protective energy instantly, and relationships with guardians who never sleep.

The key is consistent practice before crisis arrives. You cannot learn breath shielding while panic floods your nervous system. You cannot establish ancestral relationship when disaster has already struck. These techniques demand repetition until they become instinct—spiritual muscle memory that activates without conscious thought.

Start tonight. Ground yourself. Choose one method that resonates: assemble a protection amulet, practice the mirror gesture until your fingers move automatically, or speak to your ancestors while lighting a white candle. Master that single technique completely before adding others.

Depth always outperforms breadth in protection work.

Your spirit requires defense as much as your body needs shelter. The forces that move through this world—human malice, spiritual interference, accumulated negativity seeking vessels—do not respect wishful thinking or good intentions. They respect boundaries maintained through knowledge, materials properly worked, and will consistently applied. Fortifying your spirit is only half the equation. The other half lives in the spaces you inhabit daily—your home, your workplace, the threshold between public and private worlds.

What comes next moves beyond defending yourself to **defending the ground beneath your feet**.

Chapter Eight

Cleansing and Clearing: Removing Obstacles and Stagnant Energy from Your Life

Purifying Your Personal Space: Home Cleansing Rituals

Preparing for Cleansing

Most practitioners fail their first home cleansing not because they chose the wrong herbs or burned the wrong candle, but because they walked into sacred work with fractured attention and unclear purpose.

They decided to cleanse "whenever I get around to it" while mentally juggling grocery lists and work deadlines, grabbed random supplies they'd heard about somewhere, then wondered why their space felt exactly the same three days later. **Preparation isn't preliminary—it's already the work.** When you approach a home cleansing with genuine readiness, you're not simply collecting ingredients. You're entering into conversation with forces that respond to coherence, not wishful thinking. Your intention needs the clarity of a surgical cut: not "I want good vibes" but "I am removing all stagnant energy accumulated from the argument on Tuesday and the financial anxiety that's been feeding itself in my bedroom corner." Write it down. Say it aloud until the words lose their vagueness and become declarative truth.

Timing matters because energy moves in cycles whether you acknowledge them or not. The **waning moon**—from full to new—pulls things away from you, making it the natural ally for cleansing and banishment work (Otherworldly Oracle, 2020). Saturdays traditionally belong to Saturn's restrictive, binding energy, useful for serious removals (Penczak, 2014; Yusuf, 2020).

But if your home feels suffocated by stagnant energy right now, waiting two weeks for perfect planetary alignment means living in spiritual sludge for fourteen more days.

Gathering materials requires discrimination. You need a **new broom** that's never touched your floors, designated specifically for spiritual sweeping. **Salt**—cheap, abundant, irreplaceable. White candles as focal points. At least one cleansing herb you can identify by scent: cedar, rosemary, or dried sage. A bowl for salt water.

Nothing exotic, nothing expensive. The question isn't whether you have access to obscure roots shipped from distant suppliers. It's whether you're prepared to show up fully present, with clear intention and respect, to do work that will actually shift the energy you're living in.

Hoodoo Cleansing Techniques

Floor washes are the oldest continuous cleansing practice in Hoodoo, carried directly from African traditions where spiritual and physical cleaning merged into a single act. You're not mopping. You're rewriting the energetic foundation of your home from the ground up.

The traditional method starts with salt water in a bucket—roughly a handful of salt dissolved in warm water. Add your cleansing herbs: **hyssop** for deep purification mentioned in biblical Psalms, **basil** for clearing negativity, or **pine** for its sharp cleansing bite. Strain out plant material if you're working on finished floors. Speak your intention directly into the water: "This wash removes all stagnant energy, all lingering conflict, all spiritual debris from this home." Start at the back of your house and work toward the front door, pushing everything out. This directional flow isn't symbolic—you're physically moving energy along a clear path of exit.

Never step over wet floor wash. Walk around it or wait for it to dry.

Smoke cleansing works differently, addressing what clings to walls and saturates fabric that floor washes can't touch. Cedar, rosemary, or dried sage burned in a fireproof bowl produces smoke you direct with intention and a feather or your hand. Move through each room in a **counter-clockwise direction**, paying particular attention to corners where energy stagnates, closets that stay closed, and spaces behind furniture. The smoke doesn't magically absorb negativity—it disrupts settled patterns, breaks up dense pockets, and creates movement in places that have gone spiritually stale.

Combining methods creates depth that single techniques can't match. Floor wash first to clear the foundation, smoke cleansing second to address what rises above ground level, then **threshold protection** using a line of salt mixed with red brick dust across doorways to prevent anything from drifting back inside. Each layer reinforces the others, building cumulative spiritual pressure that doesn't just clear your space temporarily but establishes lasting energetic hygiene.

Maintaining a Cleansed Space

Cleansing once doesn't create a sanctuary. Regular upkeep does. Most people treat spiritual cleansing like deep cleaning—an intensive burst when things feel unbearable, then nothing until crisis hits again. That approach leaves you constantly catching up to accumulated density rather than maintaining clarity.

Weekly maintenance should become as routine as taking out trash. A quick floor wash with salt water and a few drops of *Florida Water* takes fifteen minutes and prevents the buildup that requires hours to address later (The Life Potion, 2025; Rock Collage, 2024; The Divine Feminine, 2021). Pick a day—Friday works well traditionally, preparing your home for the weekend's rest—and stick to it. Consistency matters more than intensity here. You're not performing deep spiritual surgery every week; you're preventing conditions that require it.

Watch for specific signs that energy is accumulating faster than your regular schedule addresses. Unexplained irritability that seems location-specific rather than following you everywhere suggests stagnant pockets developing in particular rooms. Sleep disruption without medical cause often indicates bedroom energy needs immediate attention. Arguments that escalate inexplicably when everyone enters a specific space signal that room is holding unresolved tension. Objects falling repeatedly in the same area aren't clumsiness—they're physical manifestations of energetic disturbance.

Threshold maintenance requires particular vigilance because doorways take constant spiritual traffic (Push Black Spirit, 2024; Original Botanica, 2023; Homes & Gardens, 2023). That salt and red brick dust line you laid down degrades, gets tracked away, needs refreshing. Red brick dust is a traditional spiritual material associated with protection and guarding thresholds, commonly used in Hoodoo and other folk spiritual traditions, often placed across doorways or along property boundaries to ward off negativity and strengthen spiritual boundaries. Check monthly at minimum, immediately after visitors who brought heavy energy, and always after conflict.

Season changes demand deeper work. The energetic shift between winter and spring, summer and fall creates natural openings for accumulated debris to release more easily. Plan quarterly intensive cleansings timed with equinoxes and solstices, using the earth's own rhythm to amplify your efforts. This isn't superstition—it's working with observable energetic tides rather than against them.

Your home either supports your spiritual work or undermines it. There's no neutral ground.

• • •

Restoring Personal Energy: Spiritual Baths and Rituals

Preparing for a Spiritual Bath

Spiritual baths perform a different function than your morning shower. They address what accumulates on you rather than in your environment—the exhaustion that soap doesn't touch, the residue from difficult interactions that clings regardless of physical hygiene, the slow drain of navigating systems designed to extract rather than nourish. **A spiritual bath removes what doesn't belong to you** and restores what does. You're not washing your body; you're cleansing your spiritual field using your body as the gateway.

Preparation begins with intention that reaches beyond generic "cleansing." Are you removing specific negativity from a workplace confrontation, clearing accumulated anxiety, or restoring energy after weeks of depletion? Your intention determines which herbs and materials you'll use. Write it in one clear sentence before you begin.

Gathering materials requires deliberate selection, not random accumulation. For basic cleansing, hyssop breaks up spiritual grime with remarkable efficiency. Salt draws out what needs leaving and grounds scattered energy simultaneously. Florida Water, that cologne-sharp liquid found in any botanica, cuts through psychic debris with precision. White candles provide focus and light. You'll also need fabric—a clean white cloth works—to strain herbs from bathwater, because sitting in plant matter creates distraction rather than purification.

Timing follows the same lunar logic as home cleansing. **Waning moon pulls things**

away from you, making it ideal for removal baths. New moon creates openings for restoration work. But if you're carrying someone else's anger like a coat you can't remove, waiting feels less strategic than immediate.

Creating the right atmosphere transforms bathing from routine into ritual. This isn't about aesthetics—it's about removing distraction so you can focus spiritual pressure on the work itself. Dim lighting helps. Silence or deliberate sound choices matter. Turn off notifications, lock the door, and claim uninterrupted time. Your ancestors didn't have luxury bathrooms with perfect ambiance; they had clarity of purpose and unbroken attention.

Match that.

The bath itself demands active participation rather than passive soaking. You'll speak intention over the water, address the herbs directly, and use your hands to move water over your body with purpose. Preparation isn't separate from the working—it's already establishing the container that allows spiritual forces to respond to your call.

Physical space preparation matters more than many realize. Clean your bathroom beforehand, not for cleanliness theater but because you're about to ask spiritual forces to assist removal work. Offering them a neglected, cluttered space sends contradictory signals. Scrub the tub, clear the counters, and establish basic order before requesting spiritual intervention.

Performing Energy-Cleansing Rituals

In Hoodoo tradition, spiritual cleansing baths function as deliberate interventions against energetic accumulation—the residue left by difficult interactions, draining environments, and negative influences that cling to your spiritual field. These aren't relaxation rituals. They're targeted work designed to strip away what doesn't belong to you, restoring the clarity and vitality that stagnant energy obscures.

The practice addresses a fundamental principle: negative energy doesn't simply dissipate on its own. It accumulates, particularly in areas like your solar plexus, throat, and the back of your neck, creating density that attracts more of the same. A properly executed spiritual bath removes this buildup, breaking the pattern of attraction and allowing your natural energy to flow unobstructed.

Begin your preparation separately from regular bathing. Boil water and steep your chosen herbs—hyssop works powerfully for purification—for at least thirteen minutes. Strain the mixture thoroughly using clean fabric, removing all plant matter. While the herbed water cools to a comfortable temperature, speak your specific intention over it three times. Be clear. Be direct. Vague intentions produce vague results.

Draw your regular bath at a temperature that permits extended soaking. Add the prepared herb water along with a palmful of salt. Light a white candle and position it safely where you can see the flame throughout the ritual. **Enter the bath facing the drain**. This positioning matters—you're symbolically placing yourself to release downward rather than absorb.

Once seated, take three deep breaths to establish focus. Cup water in your hands and pour it over your head nine times. Nine is an odd number that creates movement, breaking stagnant patterns. With each pour, visualize specific debris leaving: the anxiety from last week's confrontation, the depleting energy of that phone call, the accumulated weight you've been carrying. Don't generalize. Name what you're releasing.

After the ninth pour, speak your intention aloud. Not whispered, not merely thought—**spoken with authority**. Your voice carries power in this work.

Remain in the water for at least thirteen minutes. Use your hands to scrub your body from head downward, physically directing energy toward the drain. Pay particular attention to your solar plexus, throat, and the back of your neck where spiritual residue accumulates most densely. You're not just washing—you're deliberately moving energy out of your field.

When you exit, **step out facing away from the drain**, symbolically leaving what you've released behind you. This isn't optional. Do not rinse with regular water afterward—doing so negates the work you've just completed. Pat dry with a clean towel reserved specifically for spiritual work, or air-dry if practical.

Drain the tub immediately while speaking a final release statement. Some practitioners pour a splash of vinegar down the drain afterward to ensure complete energetic separation. Dispose of the candle remains outside your home. Your spiritual field has undergone intensive cleaning and requires integration time—rest for at least thirty minutes, drink water, and avoid immediately returning to draining activities.

For persistent negative energy, repeat the bath on three consecutive nights during the waning moon, when the natural current supports release and removal.

• • •

Clearing Spiritual Clutter: Techniques for Emotional and Energetic Release

Emotional Release Techniques

Emotion lives in the body first—that tightness across your shoulders after someone's jealousy lands, the knot in your stomach from an argument three days past, the heaviness in your chest you can't quite name. **Spiritual baths remove external debris, but emotional residue requires direct release through your own action.** You must move it out yourself.

Start with a release journal kept separate from daily writing. This isn't gratitude listing or thought organization—it's deliberate purging. Write without stopping for at least **nine minutes**, putting onto paper everything you've been carrying that doesn't serve you: resentments you've been polite about, fears you've minimized, anger you've swallowed to keep peace. Don't edit. Don't make it readable. When you finish, read it aloud once in private, then burn the pages in a fireproof bowl, speaking your release intention as smoke carries the words away. Dispose of ashes outside your home, preferably at a crossroads or running water.

For emotions lodged too deep for words, **create a physical release ritual using breath and sound.** Stand barefoot on earth if possible, or on your floor with bent knees and hands pressed to your solar plexus where emotion concentrates. Breathe deeply **three times**, then on the **fourth exhale**, release sound—a sustained hum, a vowel held until breath runs out, even a scream if you're somewhere private. Let the sound carry what language can't reach. Repeat **nine times**, feeling the vibration move stagnant energy through your body and out.

Guided meditation provides structured emotional clearing for those who need direction. Sit comfortably, light a white candle, and visualize roots extending from your spine deep into earth. Mentally scan your body for areas of tension or heaviness. When you locate emotional weight, breathe into that space, visualizing it as dark smoke. With each exhale, watch that smoke travel down your roots into earth, where it transforms into neutral energy.

Perform these practices during the waning moon when natural currents support release, or immediately when emotional accumulation feels unbearable.

Energetic Clearing Practices

Once you've released what's been sitting heavy inside you, strengthen your energetic boundaries through **smoke cleansing**. This isn't just wafting incense around—it's using concentrated plant smoke to break up stagnant energy clinging to your aura and physical space. Light dried rosemary, sage, or cedar in a fireproof dish. Move smoke deliberately around your body from feet to crown using your hand or a feather, paying attention to areas that feel dense or cold. Then walk counterclockwise through each room, focusing smoke into corners where energy stagnates. Open windows before you begin so released debris has somewhere to go.

Sound healing works through vibration rather than symbolism, disrupting stuck energy patterns through resonance. While the precise physical mechanism of 'energy disruption' remains an esoteric concept, research on sound-based practices like singing bowl meditation has shown quantifiable benefits. A 2016 study in the *Journal of Evidence-Based Complementary & Alternative Medicine* observed significant reductions in tension, anxiety, and depression following such meditation. You don't need expensive singing bowls—your voice suffices. Stand in your space and hum a single sustained note, moving slowly through the room. Notice where your voice sounds muffled or strained; that's where energy has accumulated.

Keep humming there until the sound clears. Alternatively, use bells, rattles, or even spoons struck against each other. The goal is consistent vibration that breaks up density. (Goldsby et al., 2017)

Aura brushing addresses your personal energy field with surprising directness.

Stand relaxed with arms at your sides. Using your dominant hand held flat, sweep downward from the crown of your head to your feet without touching your body, staying about **three inches away from your skin**. Make deliberate brushing motions as if removing cobwebs. Focus on your solar plexus, throat, and the back of your neck. After each full-body sweep, shake your hand toward the ground to release what you've gathered. Repeat at least **nine times**. These practices won't feel dramatic while you're doing them. You might feel nothing initially, then notice hours later that the background static in your mind has quieted.

Maintaining Spiritual Clarity

Clearing spiritual clutter is only the beginning. The real power lies in **keeping it clear**.

You've done the work—released the old emotions, swept away the stagnant energy, and made room for something better. But spiritual clarity isn't a one-time achievement. It's a daily commitment. Without maintenance, the clutter creeps back in, settling like dust on a shelf you thought you'd cleaned for good. The key to lasting transformation is building simple, consistent practices that keep your spiritual space open, light, and ready for whatever comes next.

Start with your breath. **Intentional breathing** is one of the simplest yet most powerful tools for maintaining clarity (Pratt, 2025). When you feel scattered or overwhelmed, pause. Breathe in slowly through your nose, hold for a count of four, then release through your mouth. As you exhale, imagine any tension or confusion leaving your body. This isn't just relaxation—it's spiritual housekeeping. Done daily, even for just a few minutes, intentional breathing has been shown to improve mental clarity, focus, and cognitive function by increasing oxygen supply to the brain and reducing stress.

Affirmations work the same way. Speak them out loud each morning, declaring your intentions for the day: "I am protected. I am clear. I release what no longer serves me." These aren't empty words—they're declarations that shape your spiritual reality. Repeat them while dressing, brewing coffee, or lighting a candle. The more you affirm your clarity, the more you reinforce it (Wellspring Center for Prevention, 2024).

Meditation deepens the work. You don't need an hour on a cushion. Research indicates that even short bursts of daily mindfulness, as little as five to ten minutes, can significantly improve well-being, reduce depression and anxiety, enhance mental clarity, and boost attention and memory. Visualizing yourself surrounded by clean white light can be a component of such practices. This daily reset keeps your energy fresh.

Make these practices *yours*. Adapt them to fit your life. The goal isn't perfection—it's consistency. When you commit to maintaining your spiritual clarity, you ensure that the freedom you've claimed stays with you, growing stronger with each intentional breath, each spoken truth, each quiet moment of stillness.

Chapter Nine

Prosperity and Manifestation Magic: Attracting Money, Opportunity, and Success

Cultivating the Right Mindset for Abundance: Gratitude, Belief, and Aligned Action

Harnessing Gratitude

Amidst unimaginable suffering, enslaved Africans and their descendants cultivated powerful spiritual practices that transformed immense loss into resilience. This included finding gratitude for what little remained, such as the symbolic offering of three pennies, demonstrating not denial, but a profound spiritual alchemy that defied their captors' understanding.

This practice of gratitude under impossible conditions wasn't weakness or acceptance of oppression. **It was strategic magic** rooted in profound spiritual understanding: the energy you consistently hold shapes the reality you attract. Our ancestors knew that fixating on what's missing creates a magnetic pull toward more absence, while genuine appreciation for what exists—however small—opens channels for increase.

Modern practitioners often misunderstand this principle as toxic positivity or passive acceptance. They think gratitude means pretending problems don't exist or accepting injustice with a smile.

But traditional Hoodoo gratitude operates differently. **You acknowledge exactly where you are while refusing to let that current state define your spiritual frequency.** When a root worker lights a candle over three coins, thanking spirit for present resources before asking for more, she's not ignoring her empty cupboard. She's establishing herself as someone who recognizes abundance—the kind of person prosperity flows toward rather than away from. The shift from lack-consciousness to abundance-awareness changes everything about your manifestation work. Desperation repels. Appreciation attracts. Spirits respond differently to practitioners who approach with gratitude rather than grasping need, because gratitude demonstrates faith in the work before results appear.

This faith isn't blind optimism—it's operational knowledge that abundance exists and you're positioning yourself to receive it.

Three daily practices build this foundation effectively. Each morning before your feet touch the floor, name three specific things you're grateful for—not abstractions like "my health" but concrete realities like "hot water for washing" or "the rosemary growing outside my door." Throughout the day, touch your doorframe and whisper thanks when entering your home, however humble. Before sleep, hold a coin and thank it for all money that reached your hands that day, regardless of amount. These aren't mere affirmations. They're frequency adjustments that realign your spiritual broadcast to match the abundance you're calling in.

Cultivating Unwavering Belief

Gratitude establishes the foundation, but **belief powers the actual work**. You can express thanks all day, but if you don't genuinely believe your candle will draw money or your mojo bag holds protective force, you're performing empty theater. Spirits recognize the difference immediately.

This presents a genuine paradox for beginners. How do you believe in something you haven't yet experienced? How do you trust your own power when you're just learning to light dressed candles and speak petitions aloud?

Traditional practitioners solved this through small, verifiable tests that built confidence incrementally. **You don't start by trying to manifest a house—you begin with parking spaces and found coins.** An elder might tell a skeptical newcomer to dress a green candle with prosperity oil, speak a clear petition for receiving unexpected money within three days, then watch what arrives. A returned deposit. A forgotten bill in a coat pocket. Five dollars from a neighbor repaying a loan. These aren't coincidences dismissed by practitioners who understand how spiritual currents actually move through the material world.

Each small success becomes evidence. Not faith requiring you to ignore reality, but *experiential knowledge* built through repeated verification. After your third petition produces tangible results, doubt loses its foothold. After your tenth, you approach the work with entirely different energy—not hope that it might work, but operational certainty that it does work when you follow proven methods correctly.

Limiting beliefs function as spiritual blockages that divert power before it reaches your target.

A woman burning candles for financial increase while internally believing "people like me never get ahead" splits her energy between contradictory broadcasts. The candle says one thing. Her core conviction says another. Which signal do you think reaches louder?

Identifying these blocks requires uncomfortable honesty. Write down your manifestation goal, then immediately write every doubt that surfaces. "I want to attract new income" followed by "but I always mess up opportunities" or "money never stays with me" reveals the actual belief sabotaging your work. Name it clearly. Ancestral workers knew you can't transform what you won't acknowledge. That uncomfortable list becomes your actual working ground—the precise beliefs requiring intentional replacement through sustained practice and accumulated proof.

Taking Aligned Action

Belief without action remains theoretical—spiritual window shopping that produces no actual change. **Your ancestors didn't just pray for freedom; they walked toward it**, risking everything on physical movement that matched spiritual intention. Hoodoo has always demanded this marriage between unseen work and visible effort.

When you dress candles for employment but never submit applications, you're asking spirits to do all the heavy lifting while you watch from the sidelines. That's not how the partnership functions. **Aligned action means making concrete moves that reinforce what you're working for spiritually.** You burn prosperity candles and simultaneously update your resume. You carry a mojo bag for new opportunities while actually saying yes when invitations arrive. You petition for business success while physically organizing your workspace, reaching out to potential clients, and showing up consistently. The spiritual work opens doors and shifts currents; your physical action walks you through them before they close.

This creates a feedback loop that spirits recognize and amplify.

When they witness you honoring their assistance with tangible effort, they invest more heavily in your success. Traditional root workers speak of this as *proving your seriousness* —demonstrating through action a genuine commitment to the requested outcome, rather than just dabbling. Start by identifying three concrete actions supporting your current manifestation goal. If you're working for financial increase, those might be researching additional income sources, selling unused items, or asking about overtime opportunities. If you're drawing love, perhaps joining social activities, updating your appearance, or clearing physical space in your home for a partner. **Write these actions down immediately after performing spiritual work**, then complete at least one within twenty-four hours.

Timing matters here. The energy you raise during candle work or petition-setting remains active and available. Riding that momentum into aligned action amplifies both efforts exponentially. Waiting three days means starting from scratch, rebuilding energy your delay already let dissipate.

* * *

Practical Spells for Attracting Wealth and Opportunities: Step-by-Step Rituals

Foundational Spellcrafting Basics

Spellcrafting begins with **clarity of purpose**. Before you gather a single herb or light your first candle, you need to understand precisely what you're asking the universe to deliver. Vague intentions yield vague results. If you seek prosperity, define what that means: is it a specific sum of money, steady income, a new job opportunity, or relief from debt? The sharper your focus, the more direct the spiritual pathway you create.

Your intention must resonate in both your mind and your spirit.

Once you've crystallized your goal, the next step involves gathering your materials with deliberate care. Every element in a Hoodoo spell carries **symbolic and energetic significance**.

Green candles for money work, lodestones for attraction, cinnamon for swift action, pyrite for wealth manifestation—these aren't arbitrary choices. They are rooted in generations of practice, each item selected because it *works*, because rootworkers before you proved their effectiveness. As you collect these items, handle them with respect and awareness. Touch each herb, each stone, each candle, and mentally affirm its purpose in your working.

Preparing your mind and space is equally essential. You cannot walk straight from daily chaos into effective spellwork.

Cleanse your workspace using methods you've already learned: sweep away physical clutter, burn purifying herbs like sage or frankincense, sprinkle salt water around your perimeter. This creates a **sacred container** for your magic, separating ordinary reality from spiritual work.

Then turn inward. Quiet your thoughts through deep breathing. Ground yourself by visualizing roots extending from your body into the earth, anchoring your energy. This mental preparation ensures you approach your spell from a place of **calm power** rather than desperate anxiety. The difference matters profoundly—magic fueled by centered intention flows differently than magic born from fear or desperation.

With these foundations established, you're ready to work.

Money-Drawing Candle Ritual

Across generations, people facing financial crisis have sought guidance from rootworkers who understood the practical magic of prosperity. The prescribed remedy often appeared deceptively simple: a green candle, prosperity oil, and a handful of specific herbs chosen for their traditional power to attract abundance. Yet what looked like basic materials concealed profound spiritual technology.

The ritual's true power emerged not in the moment the candle was lit, but in the internal transformation it catalyzed. When someone desperate for financial relief performed this work in the privacy of their home, something shifted. Not instantly. Not magically in the fantasy sense. But **fundamentally**—a realignment of spirit and perception that opened pathways previously invisible. Desperation calcified into determination. Paralysis dissolved into action. The ritual didn't manufacture opportunities from nothing; it cleared the fog of fear that had obscured what was already there.

Traditional practitioners grasped what many beginners miss entirely. This work doesn't summon money from thin air or violate the natural order. It **aligns your spiritual frequency with abundance**, making you receptive to opportunities your desperation had blinded you to. Desperation creates energetic static—fear, lack-consciousness, frantic grasping—that repels the very prosperity you seek. The candle ritual quiets that interference, signals to helping spirits that you're ready to receive, and asks them to clear obstacles from your path.

The mechanics matter immensely.

When you dress a prosperity candle, you're not merely coating wax with oil. You're **loading that candle with concentrated purpose**, transforming ordinary material into a spiritual beacon. Each herb carries specific energetic properties verified through generations of practice: basil for steady income, cinnamon for swift movement, pyrite chips for wealth attraction. The oil binds these elements together, serving as the carrier wave for your intention. As you carve symbols into the candle's surface—dollar signs, your name, specific amounts—you're *inscribing your desire into physical form*, creating a tangible anchor for spiritual work.

Your emotional state during this ritual determines everything. You cannot burn a candle for abundance while internally broadcasting poverty consciousness. The person who lights their green candle thinking "this probably won't work anyway" sends contradictory signals that sabotage their own effort. Root doctors understood this truth so deeply they'd refuse clients radiating doubt, knowing skepticism poisons the work before it begins. Success requires emotional alignment with your stated goal—feeling the abundance you're calling forth, not the lack you're trying to escape.

Opportunity-Attracting Mojo Bag

Mojo bags function as portable spiritual batteries—condensed focal points you carry on your body, in your purse, under your pillow. Unlike candles that burn out, these small flannel pouches work continuously, broadcasting your intention twenty-four hours daily. Their power accumulates through sustained proximity to your energy field, creating an ever-strengthening signal to helping spirits and opportunity itself.

Material selection isn't decorative. Every item placed inside creates specific resonance. For attracting opportunity, traditional practitioners combined **lodestone** (magnetic attraction), **five-finger grass** (also known as cinquefoil, for opening doors), **pyrite chips** (wealth manifestation), and a **silver dime** (to draw currency itself). These aren't symbols—they're spiritual technology verified through generations of practice. The flannel color matters too: green for money opportunities, orange for general success, gold for advancement. (Candlin, 2021) (Chaparral Roots, 2022)

But here's where beginners stumble: they stuff everything promising into one bag, creating confused spiritual static rather than coherent signal.

An opportunity mojo requires focused intention. Choose three to five items maximum, each selected for clear purpose. Add a personal concern—a strand of your hair or your name written on parchment nine times—to tie the bag's work directly to you. Root doctors called this "personalizing the spirit," ensuring the attracted opportunities flow to you specifically, not diffused into the universe generally.

Activation transforms inert materials into living spiritual tools. Hold the assembled bag in both hands. Speak your intention aloud with absolute clarity: "This mojo brings me career opportunities that use my skills and pay well." Not "I hope" or "maybe"—use a declarative statement. Breathe onto the bag three times, feeding it your life force. Dress it with prosperity oil while visualizing doors opening, phones ringing, emails arriving with offers.

Maintenance determines longevity. Weekly feeding—a few drops of matching oil, whispered reinforcement of your goal—keeps the mojo charged. Sleep with it under your pillow for three nights monthly to deepen the connection.

When opportunities start manifesting, offer gratitude by leaving three pennies at a crossroads, acknowledging the spirits who cleared your path (Yronwode, 2002).

When the work fails, it's usually neglect. A mojo shoved in a drawer and forgotten loses power like an unwatered plant withers. Or the carrier harbors secret disbelief, undermining their own petition through persistent doubt. The bag reads your energy constantly—feed it attention, belief, and regular reinforcement to maintain its strength.

Prosperity Bath for Manifestation

Prosperity baths work from the outside in, reversing common spiritual logic. Immersing your physical body in ritually prepared water directly strips away accumulated energetic debris that blocks financial flow. Every rejection, overdue bill, and anxious money conversation leaves a residue on your spiritual body, an invisible film that repels opportunity like oil repels water.

Traditional root workers understood this viscerally, prescribing baths before major financial moves—job interviews, business openings, loan applications. Just as you wouldn't enter sacred space filthy, you don't petition for prosperity while spiritually grimy.

Gather your materials with intention. You need **basil**, traditionally associated with money drawing, **chamomile** for attracting luck, and **cinnamon** to accelerate financial gain. Add a splash of **Florida Water** or simple cologne if you have it—the alcohol carries prayers upward while the fragrance signals spiritual cleanliness. A white or green candle anchors the work.

Brew your bath water deliberately. Pour boiling water over your herbs in a heat-safe bowl, speaking your intention clearly as steam rises. "I cleanse all obstacles from my path. Money flows to me freely and joyfully." Let it steep until cool enough to handle, then strain out the plant matter. Some workers save the herbs to bury at a crossroads later, releasing blocked energy permanently.

Bathe normally first—soap, shampoo, the mundane cleansing. Prosperity work begins on a physically clean body. Then pour your prepared herbal water over yourself from the neck down, starting at your crown and letting it cascade naturally. *Never* pour spiritual bathwater over your head unless specifically directed; you risk washing away your own clarity and personal power.

As the water touches your skin, **visualize financial blockages dissolving**. See old failures, shame about money, and scarcity thinking washing down the drain. Speak your petition aloud: what you're calling in, why you deserve it, how you'll use it wisely. The ancestors and spirits listening respond to specificity, not vague wishes.

Air dry if possible, letting the herbal essence absorb into your skin. Light your candle and sit with it briefly, feeling the shift in your energy. You should feel lighter, more magnetic, ready to receive. Dispose of remaining bathwater by tossing it toward the rising sun—east—to carry your petition forward into new beginnings.

Repeat this bath for three, seven, or nine consecutive days when facing significant financial challenges. Consistency builds spiritual momentum that single workings cannot achieve.

• • •

Maintaining a Prosperous Life: Integrating Manifestation Practices into Daily Routine

Daily Gratitude Rituals

Start each morning by naming three specific things you're grateful for before your feet touch the floor. Not vague appreciation—*concrete* acknowledgment. "I'm grateful the rent is paid through March fifteenth. I'm grateful my car started yesterday in the cold. I'm grateful Sarah referred that client last week." Speak them aloud. Your voice carries intention into the physical world, making gratitude more than fleeting thought.

Keep a small notebook beside your bed dedicated solely to this practice. Write the date, then list your three items in present tense: "I am grateful for..." The act of writing engages your body in the ritual, creating muscle memory that reinforces the spiritual work. Within two weeks, your brain begins scanning for gratitude opportunities throughout the day rather than dwelling on lack. This rewiring isn't metaphor—it's a documented cognitive shift that opens you to noticing abundance already present (Fox et al., 2015).

Before meals, pause for fifteen seconds. Look at your plate and acknowledge the chain of prosperity that brought this food to you: money earned, transportation available, a functioning stove, clean water. Speak one sentence of thanks. This transforms eating from mindless routine into **prosperity affirmation** three times daily, anchoring abundance consciousness in your most consistent habit.

Create a gratitude jar using a clear glass container. Each Friday evening, write one financial blessing from the week on a small paper slip—an unexpected refund, a bill smaller than expected, someone buying you coffee, finding five dollars in an old jacket. Fold it once and drop it in the jar. Watch physical evidence of prosperity accumulate.

When doubt creeps in during difficult weeks, read through past slips. This practice trains your attention on what's working rather than what's broken, shifting the energetic frequency spirits and opportunities respond to.

End each day by telling your ancestors thank you for three things before sleep. They hear you. This creates **reciprocal flow**—gratitude flowing backward to those who paved your path, blessings flowing forward to you. The circuit completes itself through acknowledgment.

Consistency matters more than perfection. Miss a day, start again the next. These aren't obligations—they're invitations to partnership with abundance.

Aligning Actions with Intentions

You won't get this perfect, and that's precisely the point. Hoodoo work thrives through sustained effort rather than flawless execution, through showing up repeatedly rather than performing one pristine ritual. The ancestors honored fumbling beginnings—they knew survival depended on trying with imperfect knowledge rather than waiting for mastery that might never come.

Some weeks your morning gratitude practice will feel mechanical, the words flat in your mouth. Light your prosperity candle anyway. Other times you'll forget to feed your mojo bag for three days straight, or you'll skip your basil tea because you overslept. **Return to the practice without self-punishment.** Guilt creates the same energetic static as doubt—it interferes with the signal you're broadcasting.

When financial pressure intensifies, your first instinct will be abandoning the spiritual work to focus solely on "practical" solutions. This is exactly backward. Desperation without grounding generates frantic energy that repels opportunities and clouds judgment. The fifteen minutes you spend at your ancestor altar or dressing a candle aren't stolen from job applications—they're what makes you *magnetic* to the right opportunities rather than desperately grasping at wrong ones.

Expect plateaus where nothing visible shifts for weeks. Roots take time establishing themselves underground before anything breaks the surface. Spiritual work operates on rhythms that don't match your bank statement's due dates. This tests your faith more than any dramatic obstacle, because boredom lacks the clarity of obvious challenge.

Track small shifts: an unexpected helpful conversation, finding exact change when you need it, a sudden idea that solves a problem. These aren't coincidences—they're evidence the work is moving. Hoodoo changes you first, then circumstances respond to your transformation.

When doubt arrives—and it will—speak your intentions aloud anyway. Feed your lodestone. Sweep your threshold. Let the physical actions carry you when belief wavers. Your hands remember what your mind questions.

Progress looks like returning after you've stopped. It looks like lighting one candle when you planned an elaborate ritual but life intervened. **Sustainability defeats perfection** every time, because magic requires your presence far more than your performance.

Adapting Practices for Growth

Prosperity work never finishes—it evolves alongside your circumstances, requiring honest assessment and strategic adjustment. Every three months, pause to evaluate what's actually producing results versus what you're continuing from habit. That mojo bag you've carried for six months might need complete reconstruction with fresh materials if your financial situation has shifted. The candle work that opened job opportunities becomes less relevant once you're employed; now you need rituals supporting salary negotiation or client retention.

Track patterns ruthlessly. Which practices preceded tangible shifts—the callback, the unexpected check, the helpful introduction? Which feel like empty repetition? Hoodoo demands pragmatism inherited from ancestors who couldn't afford wasted effort. If your

Tuesday prosperity bath hasn't moved anything in two months, either your intention needs sharpening or that particular method doesn't resonate with your spiritual frequency right now.

Life changes require corresponding magical adjustments.

A new job means different threshold protection for your workspace. Moving apartments demands complete reconsecration of your prosperity altar with materials reflecting your current goals rather than outdated ones. Marriage or partnership introduces another person's energy into your financial magic—their doubt can undermine your workings unless you address it directly through protective boundaries or include them in the practice.

Add new elements gradually when growth stalls. If you've mastered candle work and mojo bags, perhaps it's time for crossroads offerings or working with ancestral money wisdom through genealogical research. Maybe your practice needs planetary timing you've previously ignored, or specific roots like **Irish moss** for business growth. *Expansion happens through deepening existing knowledge first*, then carefully layering additional techniques. (Yronwode, 2002)

The real skill emerges when you recognize that your prosperity magic must breathe with your reality—tightening during crisis, lightening during abundance, transforming as you transform. What worked during desperate unemployment won't serve you building generational wealth. Different seasons demand different seeds.

Chapter Ten

Building Personal Power: Spells and Practices for Confidence, Influence, and Magnetism

Harnessing Inner Strength: Spells for Self-Empowerment

The Power of Self-Affirmation

hen Josephine finally left the relationship that had diminished her for seven years, she discovered something unexpected: her way of speaking had profoundly shifted. She spoke softer, hesitated before offering opinions, apologized reflexively for taking up space. The abuse hadn't just lived in her memories—it had reshaped how she inhabited the world.

This erosion of self isn't dramatic. It happens through a thousand small surrenders.

Hoodoo practitioners have always understood what psychologists now confirm: **confidence isn't merely psychological**—it lives in your bones, your voice, the way you carry yourself through a room (Guyer et al., 2021). (Petty et al., 2009). When you repeatedly silence your truth, defer your desires, or absorb criticism without boundary, you're not just making emotional choices. You're performing a kind of spiritual diminishment, teaching your very essence that it doesn't deserve space, voice, or power.

Self-affirmation spells in Hoodoo work precisely at this intersection of word, intention, and self-belief. They're not empty positive thinking or wishful mantras whispered into the void. These spells are deliberate acts of reconstruction—sacred commitments spoken aloud that reshape how you move through the world. Each affirmation becomes a declaration of your intrinsic worth, a refusal to accept the stories that diminished you, and a bridge back to your authentic power.

The magic happens in the speaking itself. Your voice carries your spirit's frequency, and when you speak truth about yourself with intention and belief, you're performing spiritual architecture—rebuilding what was torn down, reclaiming what was surrendered, restoring what rightfully belongs to you.

To create your own self-affirmation spell, begin by identifying the specific quality you wish to reclaim or strengthen: confidence, worthiness, courage, or clarity. Write a simple, present-tense statement that declares this quality as already yours. "I speak my truth with clarity and confidence" works more powerfully than "I will try to be confident." Speak it aloud each morning while standing before a mirror, meeting your own gaze without flinching, allowing your voice to carry conviction even if you don't fully believe it yet.

Belief follows practice. Your spirit learns through repetition.

Rituals for Courage and Resilience

Courage is not the absence of fear, but the quiet knowing that you possess something stronger. In Hoodoo, building courage and resilience means working deliberately with spiritual forces that bolster your inner fortitude, helping you stand firm when life tests you. These practices do not promise to remove obstacles from your path. Instead, they gift you the strength to meet them without faltering.

The High John the Conqueror Root is one of Hoodoo's most revered allies for courage. This powerful root, long associated with overcoming adversity and achieving victory against overwhelming odds, carries the essence of triumph. To work with High John, obtain a whole root and anoint it with a few drops of **frankincense oil** while speaking your intention aloud: *"I am strong. I am protected. I overcome all obstacles."* Carry this dressed root in your pocket or mojo bag, touching it whenever doubt creeps in. Its presence reminds you of your inherent power, anchoring your resolve in moments of uncertainty.

For a ritual bath that fortifies the spirit, combine **hyssop**, **rue**, and **sea salt** in warm water. As you immerse yourself, visualize the water washing away all hesitation, all fear that does not serve you. See yourself emerging cleansed, surrounded by an unshakable shield of spiritual strength. Speak these words as you bathe: *"I release what weakens me. I claim the courage that is my birthright."* This simple yet profound practice prepares you to face challenges with grace, transforming your energy from vulnerable to invincible.

When you need immediate courage before a difficult conversation or daunting task, light a **red candle** dressed with **cinnamon oil**. Focus on the flame and breathe deeply, drawing its warmth into your chest. Let that heat become your inner fire, the force that propels you forward. Extinguish the candle knowing that its energy now lives within you, ready to be called upon whenever you need it most.

Embracing the Shadow Self

Within every soul dwells a shadow—those fragments of yourself you've learned to hide, the parts deemed unworthy or unacceptable by the world's gaze. Yet Hoodoo teaches us that true power springs not from denying these hidden aspects, but from acknowledging them with unflinching honesty. The shadow self holds qualities you've suppressed: perhaps anger you were taught to conceal, ambition labeled as selfishness, or vulnerability dismissed as weakness.

Shadow integration transforms these rejected pieces into sources of strength. When you reclaim what you've pushed away, you become whole—and wholeness is where authentic power resides.

Begin this work with a simple mirror ritual. Stand before a mirror in dim candlelight, allowing shadows to play across your reflection. Speak aloud three truths you've been avoiding about yourself—not in shame, but in acknowledgment.

"I am afraid." "I crave recognition." "I carry resentment." Let these words settle in the air around you. Anoint your reflection's forehead with **frankincense oil**, tracing a cross while saying: *"I see all of who I am. I accept all of who I am. My wholeness is my power."*

For deeper integration, create a **shadow acceptance mojo bag**. Into a black cloth square, place a small mirror shard (wrapped carefully in fabric), obsidian stone, and dried mugwort. Add a piece of paper bearing your name written in your own hand—your personal concern connecting the spell to your essence.

As you tie the bag closed with black cord, visualize the parts of yourself you've rejected flowing back into your center, no longer enemies but allies. Carry this bag when you need to draw upon your complete self, especially before situations requiring your full presence and authority.

This practice doesn't excuse harmful behavior or celebrate destructive patterns. Shadow work means acknowledging what exists within you so you can choose consciously how to channel those energies. The anger you've suppressed might become **righteous boundary-setting**. The selfishness you feared might transform into **healthy self-advocacy**.

Integration is the pathway to wielding your complete power with wisdom, clarity, and intention.

• • •

Commanding Respect: Practices for Influence and Presence

Harnessing Ancestral Wisdom

Personal power doesn't exist in isolation. It flows through bloodlines, through the hands that came before you, through the ancestors who survived what should have been unsurvivable.

Your grandmother carried herself with authority not because she read about confidence but because she stood on the shoulders of those who refused to be broken. This is the truth Hoodoo has always known: commanding presence requires more than individual will. It requires ancestral connection. When you walk into a room and feel every eye assess you, when you speak and wonder if your words carry weight, you're experiencing a spiritual question. Your ancestors knew how to move through hostile spaces with dignity intact. They understood that true influence isn't performance—it's drawing on a well deeper than your single lifetime.

Ancestral presence manifests as a felt reality in your body. You stand differently when you know your great-grandmother watches. You speak with different authority when her voice echoes through yours. This isn't metaphor—practitioners report tangible shifts in how others respond to them after establishing consistent ancestor work, as though some invisible backing suddenly becomes perceptible. For instance, practitioners have observed an increased ability to engage skillfully with people of other ancestries after forming a more conscious relationship with their bloodline ancestors.

The mechanics are straightforward but demand sincerity. Establish a simple ancestor altar: white cloth, a glass of cool water changed weekly, a white candle. Add photographs if you have them, or simply speak their names aloud. Tell them what you need: "I need your strength in this negotiation." "I need your wisdom facing this decision." "I need your courage standing up to this person."

Before important moments, light the candle and speak directly: "Grandmothers and grandfathers, those who came before, I ask you to walk with me today. Let your strength be my strength. Let your dignity be my dignity. Let those who see me recognize the unbroken line standing behind me."

They answer through sudden certainty, through words that come from somewhere older than conscious thought, through the way your spine straightens without effort. This isn't borrowed power—it's **inherited authority** finally claimed.

Creating Charms for Influence

The quiet power of a personal talisman, often a small, unassuming object carried close to the body, can profoundly shift one's demeanor and how the world responds to you. For generations, rootworkers have employed such items as anchors for internal states, helping individuals project confidence and presence in spaces that might otherwise diminish them.

That charm wasn't decoration. It was **concentrated intention made physical**, assembled according to principles passed down through generations of Southern practitioners who understood that certain materials, properly combined and activated, alter how others perceive you. These charms function as spiritual amplifiers, translating the authority you cultivate internally into a presence others can feel even before you speak.

Creating influence charms follows specific construction principles: you need a carrier bag (red flannel for power, purple for authority), materials aligned with your intention, and words that seal the work. For a basic authority mojo, combine one whole calamus root for control of situations and conversations, a pinch of Master Root shavings for dominance and leadership, and five-finger grass to grasp opportunities as they appear. Add a small piece of parchment with your name written nine times in black ink, crossed by your specific intention written seven times: *"I command respect in all spaces."*

As you assemble these materials, speak your purpose aloud with each addition. Calamus goes in: "I speak with authority that cannot be dismissed." Master Root follows: "My presence commands attention." Five-finger grass last: "Opportunities bend toward me." Sew the bag shut with red thread, making nine stitches while repeating your core intention. Anoint the finished charm with bergamot or cinnamon oil, holding it between your palms while visualizing yourself moving through spaces with undeniable presence.

These charms work because they anchor internal shifts in external form. When you touch that bag before entering a difficult conversation, you're not relying on magic to do the work—you're **activating** the confidence you built while making it.

Wear the charm against your skin for maximum effect, typically near your heart or solar plexus. Feed it weekly by adding three drops of the same oil you used for consecration while restating your intention. The moment your fingers find it in your pocket before speaking, you remember who you are and what power you carry.

Embodied Presence Rituals

Rituals that align internal strength with external presence function through deliberate movement, spoken intention, and material anchors—turning abstract qualities into embodied practices you perform until they become automatic.

Begin with a **morning authority activation ritual** that takes three minutes but sets the foundation for how you move through your entire day. Stand barefoot before a mirror in morning light. Plant your feet shoulder-width apart, grounding into the earth as described in earlier practices. Place one hand on your solar plexus, one on your heart. Speak this declaration aloud, projecting your voice as if addressing someone across the room: "I carry the authority of my ancestors. I speak with clarity. My presence commands respect." Repeat it three times, each repetition louder and more certain. The physical stance matters as much as the words—your body teaches your spirit what it's claiming.

For situations requiring immediate presence—job interviews, difficult confrontations, public speaking—perform a quick **threshold crossing ritual**. Before entering the space, touch your solar plexus with three fingers while silently calling on ancestral support: "Those who came before me, lend me your strength." Cross the threshold with your right foot first, a deliberate choice signaling you enter as someone with purpose and power.

Weekly reinforcement comes through a candle ritual performed every Sunday evening. Dress an orange candle with cinnamon oil, stroking from base to wick while visualizing yourself commanding attention in specific upcoming situations. Write your name on parchment, circle it nine times with a pen, then place the candle atop it. As it burns, sit in meditation, feeling the qualities you wish to project—*steady authority, unshakeable confidence, magnetic presence*—settling into your bones and breath.

Between formal rituals, practice micro-adjustments: straightening your spine when entering rooms, making deliberate eye contact three seconds longer than feels comfortable, allowing silence after you speak instead of rushing to fill it. These small embodiments compound, teaching others—and yourself—that you occupy space with intention.

• • •

Developing Personal Magnetism: Attracting Opportunities and Connections

Cultivating Inner Magnetism

Magnetism begins not with personality adjustments but internal alignment—when who you are inside matches what you present outward, others respond to the coherence itself. People detect contradictions unconsciously. When you pretend confidence while feeling fraudulent, the mismatch creates static that repels connection. **Authentic magnetism** emerges when self-awareness, genuine confidence, and unforced presence converge into something others instinctively trust.

Start with a daily self-inventory, but make it concrete rather than abstract. Each evening, write three truthful statements about yourself using this structure: "I am someone who..." followed by verifiable behaviors, not aspirations. "I am someone who keeps my word when I make promises" rather than "I am someone who wants to be trustworthy." Track these for two weeks. Patterns reveal where you already embody integrity and where gaps exist between identity and action. These gaps drain magnetic presence faster than any external obstacle.

Build confidence through **competence stacking**—the deliberate accumulation of small, documented wins.

Choose one area weekly where you can demonstrate reliable follow-through: calling that difficult person back within twenty-four hours, completing morning spiritual practice for seven consecutive days, or saying no to one draining commitment. Write each completion down. These aren't affirmations but evidence, creating the internal foundation spirits recognize and amplify through Hoodoo work. Confidence built on nothing collapses under pressure. Confidence built on recorded competence becomes unshakeable.

Practice authentic presence through what root workers call **"clean conversation"**—speaking only what you mean, meaning what you speak. For one week, eliminate three common forms of verbal clutter: apologizing when you haven't caused harm, hedging statements with "kind of" or "sort of," and agreeing when you actually disagree. Notice the immediate shift in how others respond when your words carry weight because they're precise. This isn't about aggressive honesty but eliminating the static that diffuses your signal.

Combine these internal practices with a simple mirror exercise borrowed from old conjure wisdom. Each morning, meet your own eyes for a few minutes without breaking contact. Say nothing, fix nothing, judge nothing—simply hold your own gaze while breathing deeply. Most people find it challenging initially, and this discomfort often reveals where self-awareness fractures. Consistent practice builds the capacity to witness yourself clearly, the prerequisite for others seeing you clearly. When you can hold your own gaze without flinching, walking into rooms where you're underestimated becomes infinitely easier (Archer, 2025).

These aren't preparation for magnetism. They *are* magnetism itself, creating the internal coherence that makes all subsequent Hoodoo work exponentially more effective.

Manifesting Opportunities with Hoodoo

Personal magnetism, like all Hoodoo work, demands that you actually *do* the practice rather than collect techniques. You now understand the internal foundation—self-awareness, competence-based confidence, authentic presence—and you've encountered specific methods for building magnetic force through charm bags, oils, and candle work. What matters now is consistent application.

Begin tonight with whatever feels most accessible. If you have red flannel and a lodestone, start the attraction mojo. If those materials aren't available, light a honey-dressed candle and speak your intention for new opportunities while visualizing doors opening. **Small, completed actions** outperform elaborate plans never enacted. Our ancestors didn't wait for perfect conditions or complete knowledge—they worked with what they had, trusting that sincerity and follow-through mattered more than flawless execution.

Track your results in writing, because memory distorts what actually happens. Note when you perform workings, what materials you used, and any shifts you observe within the following week—unexpected invitations, strangers initiating conversation, opportunities appearing where none existed before. This documentation serves two purposes: it reveals what techniques work best for your specific energy, and it builds the experiential evidence that transforms hopeful belief into unshakeable certainty.

After three months of recorded practice, you'll possess knowledge no book can provide.

Feed your magnetism work weekly. Mojo bags require oil, lodestones need magnetic sand, and candles benefit from being relit on consistent days—Fridays for attraction, Wednesdays for communication and connection. This regular attention creates cumulative spiritual pressure that isolated workings cannot match. **Consistency trumps intensity** in building genuine magnetic presence.

Combine spiritual work with material action, always. Carry your dressed mojo to networking events. Schedule that difficult conversation after performing commanding presence work. Apply for opportunities during the same week you're running attraction candles. Magic opens pathways, but you must walk through them. Spirits amplify effort, not replace it.

As your practice develops, you'll notice magnetism functioning less like something you perform and more like something you embody.

Strangers respond differently. Conversations flow with less effort. Opportunities find you with increasing frequency. This shift signals that the work has moved from external technique into internal transformation—the ultimate goal of all Hoodoo practice. You're building something that will serve you for years, not weeks. Personal power isn't a single working but a sustained practice that compounds over time, strengthening with each candle lit, each charm fed, each moment you choose authentic presence over performance.

The ancestors who developed these methods survived by wielding exactly this kind of practical magic, and their wisdom now flows through your hands. Move forward with both confidence and humility. Trust what you've learned while remaining open to what experience will teach. Your magnetism grows not from perfection but from sincere, consistent practice that honors both the tradition and your own unfolding power.

Chapter Eleven

Creating Your Own Rituals: Designing Personalized Magic for Your Unique Needs

Understanding the Fundamentals of Ritual Design

Identifying Core Intentions

woman once told me she'd performed the same money spell seventeen times, letter-perfect each round, yet remained perpetually broke. When I asked what she wanted, she said "more money." When I pressed for specifics—how much, for what purpose, by when—her eyes went blank. She'd been casting spells into fog.

Hoodoo doesn't work with vague yearnings. **It demands brutal clarity.** (N/A, 2024)

You cannot light a green candle for "better finances" and expect results any more than you could give someone directions to "somewhere nice." Spirits and natural forces need coordinates. When you say "I need protection," protection from what? The universe contains infinite threats; which one are you addressing tonight?

This precision isn't pedantic—it's the difference between power and performance. Every ingredient you choose, every word you speak, every gesture you make either reinforces a singular intention or scatters your energy across contradictory desires. Our ancestors, working under enslavement with their lives depending on effective magic, couldn't afford ambiguity. Neither can you.

The work begins before you touch a single root or light a candle. It starts with interrogating yourself until the comfortable lies dissolve and what remains is uncomfortably specific. Not "love" but "clarity about whether this relationship serves my growth." Not "success" but "the promotion to senior analyst by March fifteenth."

Clarity feels exposing because it commits you to wanting something specific enough to fail at.

But this vulnerability is where power lives. Most people prefer the safety of vague intentions because specific ones can be proven wrong. Hoodoo offers no such shelter.

Choosing Symbolic Elements

Once your intention crystallizes, you face the next essential question: which materials carry that precise energy? Practitioners new to Hoodoo often reach for what appears mystical instead of what actually works. They collect pretty things rather than potent ones.

Every element must speak directly to your goal. Colors aren't decoration. Green draws money and growth because generations of rootworkers documented those results. Red pulls love, lust, and vitality—not because it "feels" passionate, but because it broadcasts that specific frequency. Yellow brings clarity and communication. Purple commands power and spiritual elevation. These aren't suggestions. They're verified correspondences.

The same precision governs herbs and roots. **Basil protects and attracts money**—not vague wellness or general abundance, but those two specific outcomes. **High John the Conqueror root** overcomes obstacles and builds confidence when facing difficult situations. **Devil's shoestring** tangles enemies and prevents you from being tripped up or crossed. Each carries power accumulated through seasons of growth and verified through use.

When you select materials, you create an energetic signature that spirits and natural forces recognize instantly.

Every addition either amplifies your singular intention or introduces static that weakens the entire working. This means resisting the impulse to include everything that seems relevant. A protection mojo doesn't require seven herbs—it needs the *right* ones, chosen because their documented properties address your specific threat. Three ingredients selected with precision outperform ten added from anxiety.

Objects carry equal weight. A key in a mojo bag doesn't vaguely symbolize "opening doors"—it literally represents unlocking the specific barrier you named. A lodestone doesn't attract abstract blessings; it draws exactly what you feed it to draw, whether customers, lovers, or luck in gambling.

Your materials are active participants, not props. Choose them like a surgeon selects instruments, not like someone decorating an altar for photographs. The work demands that precision.

Crafting a Ritual Framework

Personal mastery over materials means nothing without understanding *why this matters.* Without strong ritual design, practitioners burn through supplies, grow frustrated with inconsistent results, and eventually abandon practices that should be working.

Hoodoo survived because it produced verifiable outcomes for enslaved people who had nothing else. They couldn't afford symbolic gestures; protection, love, and justice needed to tangibly shift circumstances (Hall, 2017; Kelly, 2019; Simmons, 2000). Precise ritual structures emerged, channeling spiritual force with maximum efficiency because their very survival depended on the work. The sequence, rhythm, and order of operations were critical, determining whether a working held or scattered.

Modern practitioners face different threats, but the principle holds. This isn't about aesthetically pleasing altar displays—it's about constructing workings that hold together under spiritual pressure and deliver tangible transformation. Each element must serve a clear function: opening the work, building momentum, directing energy toward the target, sealing the results. Skip a step or muddle the sequence, and the power dissipates before reaching its intended destination. **Ritual structure acts as the container that prevents your intention from leaking away into the ether.**

Begin with the opening: setting sacred space, stating your purpose aloud, lighting your first candle. This signals transition from ordinary time into sacred work, creating a boundary between the mundane world and the spiritual realm you're about to engage.

The middle builds energy methodically. Layer your ingredients with intention—each herb added, each word spoken, each gesture performed amplifies what came before. This isn't random assembly; it's deliberate accumulation of spiritual force directed toward one precise outcome. Pay attention to rhythm here: rushed work scatters power, while excessive pause allows momentum to dissipate.

Close with authority. Seal the working with oil, tie the final knot, speak the closing prayer that releases your intention into the universe. **The closing determines whether your work continues generating results or simply fades.** Thank the spirits who assisted, extinguish your candles in the proper order, and let the ritual settle.

Your personal style emerges within this framework, not by abandoning it.

• • •

Adapting and Personalizing Existing Rituals

Understanding Ritual Elements

Most practitioners assume rituals function as fixed scripts requiring exact replication. That misunderstanding has kept more people stuck in ineffective practice than any other misconception.

Hoodoo survived precisely because our ancestors adapted constantly, transforming remembered African practices with American plants, evolving urban methods when rural land became inaccessible, and improvising materials under conditions where possession of certain herbs could mean death. The tradition you're learning never relied on rigidity—it thrived through intelligent flexibility.

Rituals contain **structural elements** and **flexible elements**, and knowing which is which determines whether your adaptations strengthen the work or gut it entirely.

The structural elements carry the ritual's actual power. **Intention** forms the foundation—the specific outcome you're directing energy toward must remain razor-sharp regardless of what else shifts. A prosperity mojo retains its core function whether you construct it on a Thursday during the waxing moon or Sunday afternoon when that's what your schedule allows, but only if the intention stays precisely focused on drawing money for rent, not vague financial improvement.

Directional movement matters equally. Drawing work moves clockwise or toward you;

banishing work moves counterclockwise or away. Reversing this flow reverses the outcome. When you stir prosperity oil into bathwater, the clockwise motion isn't theatrical—it's the difference between drawing abundance and scattering it.

Symbolic correspondence between materials and intention creates the third structural pillar. You can't substitute black candles for white in cleansing work and expect identical results. Color carries specific frequencies verified across generations. Green draws money because that correspondence holds documented power; swapping it for purple because you prefer the shade breaks the energetic circuit entirely.

But flexible elements allow tremendous creativity.

Timing enhances work without being absolute—Friday Venus energy amplifies love magic beautifully, but a protection spell cast on Tuesday when you're being spiritually attacked works far better than waiting for optimal planetary alignment while hemorrhaging energy. *Specific materials* within the correct category adapt readily. High John root powerfully overcomes obstacles, but if you can't access it, galangal root carries similar conquering energy and works when charged with clear intention. *Ritual length* and *personal gestures* remain entirely yours to determine. Ancestors working in quarters spoke brief petitions; contemporary practitioners with private space can extend candlelit focus for hours. Both approaches succeed when the structural elements hold firm.

Understanding this distinction transforms adaptation from guesswork into precision, allowing you to bend practice to your circumstances without breaking the spiritual mechanics that make it function.

Techniques for Personalization

Caroline needed an employment ritual but worked night shifts in a hospital where candle-burning was impossible. She'd found a traditional Friday afternoon working requiring sustained focus over a dressed green candle, specific oils, and uninterrupted time—none of which her life could accommodate.

Rather than abandon the work, she identified which elements carried the ritual's actual power and which could bend. The **core intention**—securing a specific nursing position at a local clinic—remained non-negotiable. The **symbolic materials**—green for financial stability, basil for employment, lodestone for magnetic attraction—stayed because those correspondences hold verified power. The **directional movement**—clockwise stirring, candle dressed from bottom to top—preserved the drawing energy essential to manifestation work.

What she adapted: timing shifted from Friday afternoon to her only private hour on Wednesday morning. Candle work transformed into a dressed vigil light she could tend briefly each day rather than one sustained burning. The oil application moved from elaborate anointing to three deliberate touches—forehead, heart, palms—while speaking her petition. Her fifteen-minute morning practice replaced the traditional hour-long working.

She got the position within three weeks.

The structural integrity held because Caroline understood something crucial: *personalization strengthens rituals when it serves your genuine circumstances rather than convenience masquerading as necessity*. Start by writing your exact intention in one brutally honest sentence. Not "better work situation" but "I will secure the clinic position at Memorial by March 15th." This precision anchors everything that follows.

Next, identify which symbolic elements your intention absolutely requires. Money work needs green or gold and materials that carry documented prosperity power—basil, cinnamon, pyrite, lodestone. You can choose *which* of these, but you can't eliminate the category entirely and expect results. Then assess your realistic constraints without apology or shame. A single parent working doubles has different temporal resources than someone with private space and flexible schedules. Ancestors working in plantation quarters adapted constantly—your studio apartment or chaotic household demands equal creativity, not identical methods.

Build your ritual around **structural elements first**: correct symbolic materials for your intention, proper directional movement, and specific petition spoken with authority.

Then adapt timing, duration, and secondary gestures to fit your actual life. The mistake most practitioners make is inverting this process—choosing convenient timing and available materials, then hoping intention compensates. It doesn't. Power flows through proper correspondence between materials and goals, amplified by your circumstances rather than fighting them. Caroline succeeded because she preserved what mattered and adapted what could bend. Her Wednesday morning practice honored both the tradition's proven mechanics and her real limitations, creating sustainable magic that worked *with* her life instead of requiring a different one.

• • •

Mastering Correspondences and Intuition in Ritual Crafting

Understanding Magical Correspondences

Correspondences are not arbitrary; they amplify natural energetic signatures. **Salt purifies by preserving**; red attracts attention through its association with life force. These are documented patterns, not symbolic games.

Master core color correspondences as foundational vocabulary. Green signifies money and growth, resonating with plants. Black absorbs negativity and protects by 'swallowing' light. White amplifies spiritual connection and purification with reflective clarity. Red draws love, passion, and visibility, representing attention and heat. Grasping their underlying principles is more vital than rote memorization.

Numbers gain power from repetition and cultural encoding. **Three signifies physical manifestation**, seven spiritual perfection, and nine cycle completion. Three candles over three nights build momentum. Seven days of work engages planetary influences. Nine knots in cord magic seal a working completely.

Elements ground work in natural law: **earth** for stability and money, **water** for emotional work and cleansing, **fire** for transformation and rapid change, **air** for communication and clarity. Align rituals with your need; financial petitions require earth energies like salt or dirt, not merely isolated candles.

Test correspondences through small workings before relying on them for urgent needs.

Building a Correspondence Toolkit

Begin by listing the core intentions you work with most frequently. **Protection, money, love, clarity, and removing obstacles** cover the vast majority of effective work. Each demands its own material signature.

For protection, assemble black salt, angelica root, devil's shoestring, iron filings, and red brick dust. Black absorbs unwanted energy. Angelica creates guardian barriers. Devil's shoestring tangles hostile intent before it reaches you. Iron repels malicious forces through spiritual density they cannot penetrate. These five form the skeleton of defensive work; additional materials enhance but don't replace its foundation.

Money work requires green candles, basil, cinnamon, lodestone with magnetic sand, and pyrite.

Green resonates with growing currency. Basil draws prosperity through its expansive nature. Cinnamon accelerates financial movement. Lodestone magnetically attracts opportunity when fed regularly. Pyrite mirrors gold's energy without requiring precious metal. Keep these materials separate from other workings; **financial energy should not**

mix with banishing or emotional components.

Assemble your toolkit through deliberate acquisition, not impulsive accumulation. Purchase one category completely before moving to the next. Master protection materials through repeated small workings—threshold dressings, quick sachets—before collecting love herbs you might use twice yearly. Depth always defeats breadth.

Document each material's behavior in your specific hands.

Basil might work sluggishly for your neighbor but explosively for you. Cinnamon could burn too hot in your workings, requiring reduced quantities. These variations matter more than published correspondence tables because **your energetic signature interacts uniquely with each substance.** Create a physical reference: index cards listing each material's verified uses, your personal results, and combination notes. Write "Angelica plus salt at threshold—noticed effect within six hours" instead of vague claims about spiritual protection. Specific observations build genuine knowledge that adapts to future needs.

Store materials in glass containers labeled with acquisition dates. Herbs lose potency; dried basil works optimally within eighteen months. Lodestones require monthly feeding. Personal concerns demand immediate use or careful preservation. Your toolkit is living relationship, not static collection. Review quarterly what actually gets used versus what gathers dust.

Three frequently-deployed materials outperform thirty neglected ones. Hoodoo rewards focused competence, not spiritual hoarding.

Developing Intuitive Ritual Skills

Your intuition is the quiet voice that knows which herb calls to your spirit before logic can explain why. In Hoodoo, this inner knowing isn't a luxury—it's a fundamental tool, as essential as any root or stone you'll ever work with. While correspondences provide the map, **intuition guides your actual steps**, revealing which path through the territory serves your specific needs.

Developing this sensitivity requires practice, patience, and trust in yourself. Start by sitting quietly with a new herb or stone before consulting any book about its properties. Hold it in your hands. Notice what sensations arise—warmth, coolness, heaviness, lightness. What emotions surface? What images or memories appear unbidden? These initial impressions are your intuition speaking, offering information that no correspondence table can provide. You might feel drawn to lavender not just for peace, but because its scent connects you to your grandmother's garden, creating a personal power link no traditional use could predict.

Daily intuition exercises sharpen this natural ability. Each morning, select three objects from your workspace without thinking—let your hand choose. Spend five minutes with each, recording whatever impressions arise without judgment or editing. Over weeks, patterns emerge. You'll notice your intuition communicating through consistent signals: perhaps tightness in your chest warns against certain materials while warmth in your palms confirms alignment.

When crafting rituals, pause before selecting each element. Ask yourself: does this truly serve my intention, or am I choosing it because a book said so? Your grandmother's wedding ring might hold more power for a love working than any traditional ingredient, because *your* connection to it runs deep. This doesn't invalidate traditional correspondences—it enriches them with personal resonance.

Trust builds gradually. Begin with low-stakes decisions, incorporating one intuitive choice into established rituals. Notice the results. Your spiritual senses strengthen through use, becoming more reliable guides as you honor them consistently.

Integrating Intuition and Correspondences

You will hesitate. You will doubt whether your work is "right" or whether you've done enough. This is normal, expected, and precisely what our ancestors faced when they adapted African practices to Southern soil without teachers standing over their shoulders.

Progress matters more than perfection because Hoodoo survived through people who acted despite uncertainty. Your first mojo bag might feel clumsy. Your candle dressing technique might lack the smoothness you've imagined. The words you speak over your workings might stumble. Do the work anyway. Each ritual you complete—however imperfect—teaches your spirit the language of this practice in ways reading never can. Competence develops through repetition, not through waiting until you feel ready.

Common obstacles will appear, and recognizing them now prevents unnecessary discouragement later. Many beginners freeze when they can't find exact ingredients, forgetting that enslaved practitioners created powerful magic with whatever grew within reach. Others abandon rituals after one attempt without visible results, expecting microwave transformation from a tradition built on patient accumulation. Some get trapped in endless research, studying correspondences instead of lighting candles, as if perfect knowledge precedes effective practice.

Address these obstacles directly.

When ingredients aren't available, apply the substitution principles you've learned—match the **energetic purpose**, not the specific name. When results seem slow, remember you're building spiritual momentum that compounds over time. When doubt paralyzes, choose the smallest possible action: light one candle, speak one prayer, carry one root. These simple acts break paralysis and reconnect you to the current of power flowing through this tradition.

You now possess the framework for creating personalized Hoodoo rituals. Your next step isn't more reading. It's gathering materials tonight and beginning, trusting that the work itself will teach you what words cannot.

Chapter Twelve

Living the Practice: Sustaining Your Hoodoo Work and Growing Your Spiritual Power

Integrating Magic into Everyday Life

Daily Rituals for Consistency

Most mornings, Hoodoo practice slips through your fingers before you're fully awake. You had every intention of lighting candles, blessing doorways, speaking to ancestors—but then the alarm screamed, coffee needed making, the phone demanded attention, and suddenly you're commuting with nothing done except vague guilt about abandoned spiritual work.

This disconnect between intention and reality is where most practitioners fail. Failure stems not from lack of knowledge, but from separating magic from daily life. Your ancestors didn't light candles at a dedicated altar every dawn because **they didn't have that luxury**. They blessed the water they carried, spoke protection over children while braiding hair, turned cooking into conjure and sweeping into spiritual cleansing. Magic survived precisely because it didn't require circumstances they couldn't guarantee.

The power in daily practice isn't dramatic transformation. It's cumulative momentum.

When you speak intention over your morning coffee—blessing it for clarity, energy, focus—you're not performing ceremony. You're **charging something you were drinking anyway** with deliberate purpose, transforming mundane routine into active magic. That thirty seconds compounds. The coffee becomes a daily touchpoint, a repeating signal to spirits and natural forces that you're consistent, present, engaged.

This consistency matters more than intensity. Inconsistent weekly candle work builds nothing. Speaking three words of gratitude each morning while washing your face—practiced without fail for months—rewires your spiritual frequency in ways occasional elaborate rituals cannot match. *Repetition creates groove*, and groove creates current, and current creates the channel through which larger workings flow with exponentially greater force.

The threshold between your bedroom and hallway already exists. Walking through it while consciously invoking ancestral protection takes five seconds and zero materials. You cross that threshold anyway.

The question isn't whether you have time for daily practice. You're already performing the actions. The question is whether you'll **wake up inside them** or keep sleepwalking through opportunities your grandmothers would have seized without hesitation.

Adapting Rituals for Modern Living

The old ways were not born in kitchens with marble countertops or apartments three stories high. They emerged from different circumstances, different landscapes, different rhythms of time. Yet **the power within them does not diminish simply because your life looks different from those who came before**. The essence of Hoodoo lies not in rigid adherence to outdated forms, but in understanding *why* each element matters and how that purpose can be honored in your present reality.

When you cannot gather dirt from a crossroads at midnight because the nearest crossroads sits beneath a traffic light, you adapt. The crossroads itself remains sacred—a place where paths meet, where choices converge, where spiritual forces gather. Perhaps your crossroads becomes the intersection near your home, visited during your lunch break when the sun stands high. **The intention and respect you carry matter far more than the exact hour**. Speak your petition with the same reverence. Acknowledge the spirits of place. The work still holds.

Consider the matter of candles, those steady flames that have witnessed countless petitions whispered in darkness. Traditional rituals often call for specific candle work over multiple days, but your life may not permit an open flame for hours at a time. Does this render the magic impossible?

Not if you understand the candle's true purpose.

Fire transforms. It releases intention into the unseen realms. It provides focus for your will. These principles remain constant whether your candle burns for seven days or seven careful intervals that fit within your schedule. **Break the work into sessions that honor both the magic and your reality**. Set your candle upon your altar each evening when you return home.

Speak your words of power. Let the flame burn while you prepare your meal, while you sit in meditation, while you ready yourself for rest. Extinguish it with gratitude, not guilt. Resume the next evening. The spell builds with each lighting, your consistency weaving the magic tighter.

Some adaptations require creativity rather than mere scheduling adjustments. Baths prepared with specific roots and herbs appear frequently in traditional Hoodoo practice, yet perhaps you possess only a shower in your small apartment. The water itself carries the blessing. **Prepare your spiritual mixture in a bowl**. Steep your herbs, speak your intentions over the water, then pour it over your head and body as you stand in the shower, letting the essence run down your skin before the clear water rinses you. The magic flows just the same.

What matters most is that you do not abandon the practice simply because the form must shift. **Adaptation is not betrayal—it is survival, continuation, honoring**. The enslaved practitioners who birthed this tradition were themselves masters of adaptation, concealing sacred work within acceptable forms, finding power in whatever materials their circumstances permitted. You walk in their footsteps when you do the same.

Maintaining Spiritual Alignment

Without consistent spiritual alignment, your magic scatters like seeds on stone. You might complete a powerful ritual on Sunday, feel the energy humming through your bones, sense the shift beginning—and then Monday arrives with its demands, Tuesday buries you in obligations, and by Wednesday you've forgotten to even light a candle. The work you began loses momentum. The spiritual current you opened starts to close.

This isn't failure. It's what happens when you treat magic as isolated events rather than ongoing relationship.

Practitioners who sustain effective work over years understand something crucial: **alignment isn't achieved once and maintained forever**. It requires daily tending, like any living thing. Your spiritual connection resembles a well more than a light switch—it must be drawn from regularly or the water grows stagnant, the path to it becomes overgrown.

The chaos of everyday life doesn't pause for your magical work. Bills still arrive. Conflicts still erupt. Exhaustion still pulls at your bones.

These forces actively work against spiritual focus, creating static that interferes with your ability to direct power clearly. Each unresolved argument carries energetic weight. Every anxious thought about money creates interference. **When your inner state resembles a hurricane, your magic reflects that turbulence**. Petitions become confused.

Candles burn unevenly. Results arrive distorted or not at all.

The ancestors knew this intimately. They maintained spiritual practice not despite daily hardship but *because of it*—protection work before dawn, petition prayers while working brutal hours, ancestor acknowledgment no matter how bone-tired they felt. **Their magic remained effective because they never allowed the connection to fully sever**, no matter what circumstances demanded.

You inherit both their methods and their necessity. Modern life may look different, but the requirement remains identical: consistent practice that keeps you spiritually centered even when everything else spins out of control. Without it, your most carefully prepared ritual becomes just theater. With it, even the simplest daily gesture carries genuine power.

• • •

Deepening Your Connection and Knowledge

Embracing Ancestral Wisdom

Ancestral connection operates through physical practice, not wishful thinking about bloodlines. Your ancestors—biological or spiritual, those who endured captivity and those who resisted it—exist not as distant mythology but as active consciousness available through deliberate invitation. They've been waiting.

Begin where enslaved practitioners began: with water and light. Historical accounts and spiritual traditions confirm that practices involving water libations and candles were central to ancestral veneration among enslaved communities, often serving as vital links to heritage and resilience. Place a white candle and a glass of fresh water somewhere you pass daily. This isn't decoration. The water conducts spiritual presence like copper conducts electricity. The candle provides beacon and warmth, the universal signal that someone is home and listening.

Speak to them. Not formally, not with baroque language you'd never use in conversation—just speak. Tell them your name. Acknowledge theirs if you know them. Say what's happening in your life. Ask for guidance on the specific problem currently breaking your sleep.

Most practitioners wait for dramatic signs and miss the whispers. Ancestral communication arrives through dreams that feel different from usual mental noise—sharper, more coherent, carrying emotional weight that lingers past waking. It surfaces as sudden knowing about which job to take or which relationship to end, the kind of clarity that bypasses rational deliberation entirely. It manifests as physical sensation: warmth at the base of your skull during meditation, pressure on your shoulders like hands resting there, unexplained comfort flooding through you when you speak their names aloud.

Consistency matters more than ceremony. Your great-grandmother who worked from dawn past dark doesn't need elaborate rituals. She needs to know you remember.

Change the water weekly—every Monday, fresh and cold. Light the candle when you need them close. Bring small offerings: coffee, a piece of cornbread, tobacco, whatever your specific lineage honored. Sit in silence for five minutes, palms open on your knees, and simply listen. The connection strengthens through repetition until ancestral support becomes as natural as breathing, their wisdom surfacing exactly when your own vision fails.

Continuous Learning and Exploration

Growth in Hoodoo is not a solitary undertaking—it flourishes through both personal study and community connection. **Expanding your knowledge** means actively seeking wisdom from diverse sources while developing the discernment to recognize what truly serves your practice. This path requires both hunger for learning and the wisdom to distinguish authentic teachings from superficial imitations.

Books remain sacred vessels of knowledge, but approach them with discerning eyes. Seek works written by practitioners who honor Hoodoo's cultural roots and demonstrate genuine understanding of its traditions. *Look for authors who cite their sources, acknowledge their teachers, and speak from lived experience rather than appropriated knowledge.* When you encounter a new text, ask yourself: Does this honor the African American heritage of Hoodoo? Does it provide practical guidance rooted in tradition? Does the author demonstrate respect for the practice's origins? These questions protect you from diluted or distorted teachings that strip Hoodoo of its authentic power.

Workshops and classes offer something books cannot—direct transmission of knowledge and the energy of shared learning. Whether in person or online, these spaces allow you to witness techniques, ask questions, and receive immediate guidance. **Choose teachers who demonstrate both mastery and humility**, who acknowledge what they don't know as readily as they share what they do. The most powerful learning often happens in the questions exchanged, the stories shared, and the collective energy raised when practitioners gather with sincere purpose.

Community engagement deepens your practice in ways solitary work cannot achieve. Connect with other practitioners through gatherings, online forums, or spiritual supply shops where rootworkers gather. These connections provide support, accountability, and the living transmission of knowledge that keeps Hoodoo vital. Yet remember: not all who claim expertise possess it. **Trust develops through observation**—watch how others practice, listen to how they speak about the work, and notice whether their actions align with Hoodoo's principles of respect and authenticity.

Integrate new knowledge slowly and intentionally. When you learn a technique or discover a new correspondence, test it within your existing practice before making it central to your work. Notice what resonates, what produces results, and what feels aligned with your spiritual path. Your practice should evolve organically, like a tree adding rings—each layer of new knowledge strengthening rather than replacing what came before.

Integrating Modern Tools and Techniques

Modern technology and traditional Hoodoo are not enemies—they're tools that serve the same purpose when wielded with clear intention. **Your ancestors adapted constantly**, substituting local herbs for African plants, hiding sacred work within Christian prayer, and transforming survival itself into spiritual practice. You honor them not by freezing their methods in amber but by continuing that adaptive intelligence.

Digital resources serve your practice when used with discernernment. Apps that track moon phases replace almanacs our grandmothers consulted. Online suppliers provide roots and herbs once gathered only by hand. Video tutorials demonstrate candle-dressing techniques that previously required in-person transmission. None of this diminishes the work—it simply extends access.

Start by identifying where technology genuinely serves your practice versus where it creates distraction. Use your phone to set daily reminders for threshold blessings or ancestor offerings. Document your spiritual work in a password-protected digital journal that travels with you everywhere. Research planetary hours through astronomy apps rather than waiting for printed tables. These applications support consistency, which matters more than romantic notions of authenticity.

When blending new-age methods with Hoodoo, maintain the tradition's core principles.

Crystal grids can amplify mojo bag work if you understand that the stones serve

Hoodoo's intention rather than replacing it. Visualization techniques borrowed from modern spirituality enhance traditional candle work when they sharpen focus rather than substitute for physical materials. **The question is always: does this addition strengthen my connection to ancestors and clarify my intention, or does it dilute the work with unnecessary complexity?**

Create a hybrid altar that honors both worlds. Place your ancestor photos beside a small digital frame cycling through family images. Burn traditional candles while playing recorded prayers or ancestral music through speakers. Use voice memos to capture spontaneous spiritual insights that once might have been lost.

Test each integration carefully. Perform a working using only traditional methods, then repeat it incorporating one modern element. Document which produced clearer results. Your practice belongs to you—technology should amplify your power, not complicate it.

* * *

Commitment to Growth and Transformation

Cultivating Consistent Practice

The power of Hoodoo doesn't live in grand, elaborate ceremonies performed once in a blue moon. It lives in the small, deliberate choices you make each morning when you wake, each evening before sleep, each moment you pause to remember your intentions. **Daily practice** transforms folk magic from something you do into something you *are*—a way of moving through the world with awareness, purpose, and spiritual alignment.

Think of your daily Hoodoo work as tending a garden. You wouldn't plant seeds once and expect a harvest without watering, weeding, or watching for growth. Your spiritual life needs the same steady attention. Start small and build naturally. Light a single candle each morning while setting your intention for the day. Keep a bowl of salt water by your door and touch it when you leave, asking for protection. Say a prayer of gratitude before your first sip of coffee. These aren't burdensome additions to your routine—they're tiny anchors that keep you connected to the sacred current running through your life.

Consistency matters more than complexity.

Discipline in spiritual practice doesn't mean rigid rules or punishing yourself when you miss a day. It means showing up with sincerity, even when the magic feels distant or you're too tired to do more than whisper a prayer. Some days, your practice will be five minutes of quiet breathing with your ancestors. Other days, it might be a full cleansing bath, candle work, and petitioning your spirits. Both are valid. What matters is that you return, again and again, to the well of your spiritual work.

Create **ritual touchpoints** throughout your day—specific moments where you pause and acknowledge the sacred. This might be as simple as stirring your morning tea clockwise while speaking your goals aloud, or touching a mojo bag in your pocket when you need courage. Over time, these small acts accumulate into profound transformation. You'll notice shifts in how you respond to challenges, how opportunities seem to find you, how protected and centered you feel even when life gets chaotic. That's not coincidence. That's the fruit of sustained practice, the evidence that your daily work is weaving real power into your life.

Embracing Lifelong Learning

Progress matters more than perfection, and this truth runs deeper in Hoodoo than in most spiritual paths. Your ancestors didn't have the luxury of waiting for ideal conditions—they worked with what they had, when they could, under circumstances that would crush most modern practitioners. You honor them by beginning where you are, not by waiting until you've accumulated every root, read every book, or feel "ready enough."

You'll forget to feed your mojo bag, miss days at your altar, or burn a candle with scattered focus. **This is normal.** Spirits recognize the overall pattern of your effort—returning after absence, attempting after failure, and showing up even when results feel distant. What matters is the thread of connection you maintain, not the illusion of flawless execution.

Life gets busy. Spiritual practice slides. Work hits plateaus that tempt you to quit.

Family members may question your path or mock your beliefs. You'll doubt results, especially during quiet periods when the magic feels dormant rather than active. These aren't signs of error, but ordinary friction every practitioner faces. The difference between those who grow and those who abandon the work lies not in avoiding these obstacles, but in moving through them with patience and trust in the process.

When overwhelm hits, strip your practice to bare essentials: one daily prayer, one weekly candle, one monthly ancestor offering. Protect that minimum fiercely. You can expand when bandwidth returns; maintaining even a small thread of connection keeps the current alive, like glowing coals rather than rebuilding a cold fire from scratch.

Deepen your knowledge continuously through books by rooted practitioners, respectful workshops, and careful documentation of your results. Stay curious, ask questions, and test methods against lived experience. Remember, you're already qualified to practice; learning and doing aren't sequential stages, but the same motion, spiraling upward as you grow into this ancient tradition that welcomes your dedication.

Balancing Magic and Mundane

Hoodoo works best when spiritual practice and physical action move together, each amplifying the other. You light prosperity candles—and you submit applications. You carry protection mojos—and you remove yourself from harmful situations. You petition ancestors for guidance—and you follow the insights they send through sudden clarity or unexpected opportunities.

This isn't duplication of effort. **Magic opens pathways; you walk them.**

Your ancestors understood this perfectly. They didn't pray for freedom while waiting passively; their spiritual work fueled their resolve. They infused spirituals with coded messages for escape, then undertook perilous journeys on the Underground Railroad to reach freedom. They carried High John root for courage, then acted with the bravery it amplified in the face of immense danger. The spiritual work prepared them internally; their physical choices manifested externally. Both mattered equally.

When these two forces align, you create what practitioners call **"clean magic"**—work that moves through reality without friction because every level of your being points the same direction. Your candle burns for employment while your resume circulates. Your honey jar sweetens a relationship while you speak with kindness. Your cleansing bath washes away old patterns while you change the behaviors that reinforced them.

Neglecting either side weakens the whole.

Spiritual work without action becomes fantasy, pleasant to imagine but powerless to shift circumstances. Action without spiritual support exhausts you, forcing change through willpower alone when you could partner with forces far greater than individual effort. The balance between these two creates the transformation you seek—not magic alone, not effort alone, but both moving as one current toward the life you're building.

This commitment to **growth through integration** is what sustains your practice beyond initial enthusiasm. You don't abandon the work when results feel slow because you understand that some changes take root beneath the surface before they bloom visibly. You trust the process your ancestors trusted, knowing that consistent spiritual practice combined with deliberate action has always been the formula for genuine power.

CONCLUSION

When you first picked up this book, perhaps a whisper of unease lingered within you, a feeling of being adrift in a world that often feels cold and uncaring. You might have sensed the invisible pull of stagnation, the sting of unwanted influences, or simply a deep, undeniable yearning for something more—a connection to a power you instinctively knew existed but couldn't quite grasp. The very idea of "magic," let alone Hoodoo, might have stirred a mix of curiosity, apprehension, and even a touch of doubt. It's natural to feel that way when stepping onto a path as ancient and potent as this one. Yet, within these pages, you sought clarity, tools to overcome feeling stuck, and practical ways to shield yourself and manifest your desires. You were looking for a compass, a guide to navigate the unseen currents that shape our lives, seeking to regain a sense of control and purpose. That initial longing, that quiet courage to explore something beyond the ordinary, has led you here, to this moment.

Now, as these final words unfold, consider how much ground you've covered, how many veils have lifted. We've walked together through the very soil where Hoodoo's roots took hold, from the vibrant spiritual landscapes of Africa to the resilient ingenuity born of the American South. You've come to understand that Hoodoo is not merely a collection of spells, but a profound testament to survival, an interwoven tapestry of African spiritual traditions, Native American botanical wisdom, and European folk elements, all adapted and transformed into a practical, results-driven folk magic. We've established that razor-sharp intention is the beating heart of all Hoodoo work, the focused energy that breathes life into every root, every candle, every prayer. You've learned that the natural world isn't just scenery, but an active partner, with herbs, roots, and minerals carrying their own ancient wisdom and power, waiting for you to connect with them respectfully.

We explored the indispensable foundations of practice: grounding yourself deeply to Earth's stabilizing current, cleansing your space and spirit of accumulated debris, and fortifying your energetic boundaries with protective practices. You now know that personal concerns—those tangible threads like hair, nails, or a handwritten name—are not just curiosities, but powerful conduits for sympathetic magic, creating direct spiritual pathways to your intentions when used with integrity and respect. From crafting robust home protections using salt and red brick dust to weaving personal shields with charged amulets, and from inviting prosperity through green candles and mojo bags to rebuilding inner strength with self-affirmation and ancestral connection, you have gathered the essential tools. We've seen that true proficiency blossoms from combining clarity of purpose with precise material selection and a disciplined ritual structure, recognizing that the tradition's strength lies in both its enduring principles and its remarkable adaptability.

Ultimately, this journey has illuminated that Hoodoo is about empowerment through direct, intentional action and a deep, reverent connection to a vibrant cultural heritage that empowers you to shape your own reality. With the knowledge now held within your hands, your life can transform into a living testament to intentionality and resilience. Envision your home becoming more than just a dwelling; it will become a fortress of peace and positive energy, where every threshold is blessed, every corner cleared, and unwelcome influences simply cannot linger. You will move through your days with an unshakeable inner confidence, a quiet authority that emanates from a spirit well-grounded and fiercely protected. The subtle shifts in energy that once felt overwhelming will become clear signals, guiding your actions and informing your choices, allowing you to sidestep negativity before it even takes root.

Opportunities, once seemingly elusive, will begin to align with your intentions, flowing toward you with greater ease because you've learned to align your spirit with the currents of abundance. You'll recognize that true prosperity isn't just about money, but about a richness of spirit, strong connections, and a life lived in purposeful flow. No longer will you feel at the mercy of circumstance; instead, you will stand as an active participant, a conscious co-creator of your reality, weaving your desires into the fabric of daily life. The whispers of your ancestors, once distant echoes, will become a comforting chorus of support, their resilience flowing through your veins, empowering you to navigate challenges with grace and fortitude. This isn't about escaping reality; it's about engaging with it more deeply, more powerfully, turning everyday actions into acts of intentional magic.

The time for contemplation has given way to the moment for action. You've absorbed the wisdom, understood the principles, and now it's your turn to make this living practice your own. Do not wait for a perfect moon phase or a forgotten ingredient. Begin right now, with what you have, where you are. Take a moment to sit quietly.

Close your eyes, and feel the connection to the earth beneath you, visualizing deep roots extending from your feet. Breathe deeply, clearing your mind. Then, find a small dish, or even just your hand, and place a pinch of salt there. With clear intent, speak aloud one specific intention you wish to manifest or one negative influence you wish to cleanse from your space. Say it firmly, as if it is already done.

Now, take that salt and sprinkle it across the main entryway of your home, sweeping it gently outward, or dissolve it in a glass of water and wipe down your doorknob, saying, "As I will it, so it is." This simple act of intentional cleansing and declaration is your first step. It is the beginning of actively claiming your space and your power, transforming the mundane into the magical through focused will and sacred material.

Let this immediate, tangible action be the bridge between knowledge and lived experience, grounding the wisdom of these pages into the reality of your day. Remember, the path of Hoodoo is a journey of continuous practice, not a destination of instant perfection. There will be days when your intentions feel scattered, days when you question your ability, or times when life's demands pull you away from your practice. This is not failure; it is simply part of the ebb and flow of life itself. The power of this tradition lies not in flawless execution, but in persistent, heartfelt engagement. You don't need to overhaul your entire life at once; simply committing to one small act of intentional magic each day—a whispered blessing over your morning coffee, a protective thought as you step out your door, a moment of gratitude to your ancestors before sleep—will build cumulative momentum.

Trust your inner knowing, that intuitive spark that drew you to these pages in the first place. Listen to the subtle whispers of the roots and the gentle guidance of your spiritual allies. You possess an inherent power, a lineage of resilience and spiritual fortitude that has been passed down through generations. Embrace this legacy. Each act of magic you perform, no matter how small, strengthens your connection to this ancient current and deepens your own innate capabilities. You are now a custodian of a profound and living wisdom, equipped to navigate your world with greater clarity and courage.

Hoodoo is more than just a collection of powerful workings; it is a profound way of life, a lens through which you see the sacred in the everyday, the whisper of the ancestors in the rustling leaves, and the divine in your own deliberate actions. It is the steadfast strength of the earth beneath your feet, the cleansing power of flowing water, and the protective fire in your spirit, all harmonized by your will. This practice is an unbroken chain of knowledge, forged in adversity and sustained by devotion, reaching back through time to empower you in the here and now. You are not walking this path alone; you walk with the wisdom of generations, with the strength of the earth, and with the incredible power that resides within your very soul. Walk tall, walk blessed, and know that the enduring power you seek has always resided within you, waiting for your touch.

As you continue on this path, remember that the journey of Hoodoo is one of constant learning and growth. Each day presents new opportunities to deepen your understanding and refine your practice. Engage with the world around you, drawing inspiration from the natural elements and the spiritual energies that surround you. Let the rhythms of the earth guide you, and allow the wisdom of your ancestors to illuminate your way. In moments of doubt, return to the foundational principles you have learned, grounding yourself in the knowledge that you are part of a rich and enduring tradition.

Embrace the challenges that come your way as opportunities for growth and transformation. Each obstacle is a chance to strengthen your resolve and deepen your connection to the magic within you. Remember that true mastery is not about perfection, but about the willingness to learn and adapt. Be patient with yourself, and trust that with each step you take, you are moving closer to the realization of your intentions.

As you weave your desires into the fabric of your daily life, take time to celebrate your successes, no matter how small. Acknowledge the progress you have made and the strength you have gained. Let each victory serve as a reminder of your power and potential. Share your journey with others, offering support and encouragement to those who walk alongside you. Together, you can create a community of like-minded individuals who are committed to living with intention and purpose.

In the quiet moments, when the world around you is still, take time to reflect on the path you have traveled. Consider the lessons you have learned and the growth you have experienced. Allow yourself to feel gratitude for the journey and for the wisdom that has been shared with you. Let this gratitude fill your heart and guide your actions, infusing your practice with love and compassion.

As you move forward, continue to explore the depths of Hoodoo, seeking out new knowledge and experiences. Let your curiosity lead you to new discoveries and insights. Embrace the unknown with an open heart and a willing spirit, knowing that each new experience is an opportunity to expand your understanding and deepen your connection to the magic within you.

Remember that the journey of Hoodoo is a lifelong pursuit, one that requires dedication, patience, and perseverance. It is a path of continuous growth and transformation, where each step brings you closer to the realization of your true potential. Embrace this journey with an open heart and a willing spirit, knowing that you are part of a rich and enduring tradition that has the power to transform your life and the world around you.

As you continue on this path, may you find strength in the knowledge that you are never alone. You walk with the wisdom of generations, with the strength of the earth, and with the incredible power that resides within your very soul. Walk tall, walk blessed, and know that the enduring power you seek has always resided within you, waiting for your touch.

REFERENCES

American Sleep Association. (2025, April 2). *The Psychology of Breathing: How Mindfulness and Breathing Intersect*. https://www.sleepassociation.org/blog/the-psychology-of-breathing-how-mindfulness-and-breathing-intersect/

Anderson, J. (2008). Conjure in the Big Apple: Cultural Preservation and the Search for Authentic African Spirituality in Twentieth-Century New York. <i>Journal of American Folklore</i>, <i>121</i>(481), 333-356.

Anderson, J. R. (2005). <i>Conjure in African American society</i>. Louisiana State University Press.

Anderson, K. (2005). *Conjure and the Spirit of the New World*. University of Illinois Press.

Anderson, K. M. (2020). Conjure, Hoodoo, and Rootwork: The Study of a Black American Folk Tradition. <i>Journal of Africana Religions</i>, <i>8</i>(1), 62-80.

Archer, S. (2025). <i>How to Practice Mirror Work (7 Step Guide)</i>. LonerWolf. Retrieved from https://lonerwolf.com/how-to-do-mirror-work/

Association of Independent Readers and Rootworkers. (2025, August 19). *Category:Personal Concerns and Magical Links*. Retrieved from https://

www.readersandrootworkers.org/wiki/
Category:Personal_Concerns_and_Magical_Links; Black Witch Coven. (2015, April 2). *Using the Personal Concerns of Others in Rootwork and Spellwork*. Retrieved from https://blackwitchcoven.com/personal-concerns-of-others-in-rootwork-and-spellwork/; Personal Concerns. (n.d.). *Personal Concerns*. Retrieved from [URL provided in snippet, but a direct, stable URL from the actual source page is preferred or null if not available. The snippet URL for 'Personal Concerns' is a vertexaisearch.cloud.google.com link. Since no better URL is available, setting it to null and providing a note].

Candlin, P. (2021). <em>The Power of Herbs in Hoodoo and Conjure</em>. Conjure and the City. https://www.conjureandthecity.com/the-power-of-herbs-in-hoodoo-and-conjure/

Chaparral Roots. (2022). <em>Magical Properties of Pyrite</em>. Chaparral Roots. https://chaparralroots.com/magical-properties-of-pyrite/

Chevalier, G., Sinatra, S. T., Oschman, J. L., Sokal, K., & Sokal, P. (2012). Earthing: Health Implications of Reconnecting the Human Body to the Earth's Surface Electrons. *Journal of Environmental and Public Health*, *2012*, Article ID 291541. https://doi.org/10.1155/2012/291541

Chireau, Y. (2003). <i>Black Magic: Religion and the African American Conjuring Tradition</i>. University of California Press.

Chireau, Y. P. (2003). <i>Black Magic: Religion and the African American Conjuring Tradition</i>. University of California Press.

Chireau, Y. P. (2006). <i>Black magic: Religion and the African American conjuring tradition</i>. University of California Press.

Crescent City Conjure. (2025, October 15). *Understanding the Roots and Traditions of Hoodoo*. https://crescentcityconjure.com/blogs/hoodoo/understanding-the-roots-and-traditions-of-hoodoo

Crescent City Conjure. (2018, January 17). *Personal Concerns in Hoodoo*. Retrieved from https://crescentcityconjure.com/personal-concerns-in-hoodoo/; Black Witch Coven. (2015, April 2). *Using the Personal Concerns of Others in Rootwork and Spellwork*. Retrieved from https://blackwitchcoven.com/

personal-concerns-of-others-in-rootwork-and-spellwork/

Crescent City Conjure. (2018, January 17). *Personal Concerns in Hoodoo*. Retrieved from https://crescentcityconjure.com/personal-concerns-in-hoodoo/; Black Witch Coven. (2015, April 2). *Using the Personal Concerns of Others in Rootwork and Spellwork*. Retrieved from https://blackwitchcoven.com/personal-concerns-of-others-in-rootwork-and-spellwork/; Personal Concerns. (n.d.). *Personal Concerns*. Retrieved from [URL provided in snippet, but a direct, stable URL from the actual source page is preferred or null if not available. The snippet URL for 'Personal Concerns' is a vertexaisearch.cloud.google.com link. Since no better URL is available, setting it to null and providing a note].

Cunningham, S. (1985). <i>Cunningham's Encyclopedia of Magical Herbs</i>. Llewellyn Publications.

Denham, A. M. (1989). <i>Folklore of Plants</i>. W. Foulsham & Co.

Dorsey, L. (2022, July 7). *Hoodoo How We Do: Psalms Are Spells*. Patheos. https://www.patheos.com/blogs/lilithdorsey/2022/07/hoodoo-how-we-do-psalms-are-spells/; Yronwode, C. (n.d.). *Psalms and Verses in Hoodoo*. Lucky Mojo Curio Co. https://www.luckymojo.com/psalms.html

Douglass, F. (1845). <i>Narrative of the Life of Frederick Douglass, an American Slave</i>. Project Gutenberg.

Fett, S. (2002). <i>Working Cures: Healing, Health, and Power on Southern Plantations</i>. University of North Carolina Press.

Foor, D. (2022). *About Ancestor Reverence: A Letter to the Editor*. Ancestral Medicine. https://ancestralmedicine.org/blog/about-ancestor-reverence-a-letter-to-the-editor/

Fox, G. R., Kaplan, J., Damasio, J., & Damasio, A. (2015). The Neural Correlates of Gratitude. <em>Frontiers in Human Neuroscience</em>, <em>9</em>, 373. https://doi.org/10.3389/fnhum.2015.00373

Goldsby, T. L., Goldsby, M. E., McWalters, M., & Mills, P. J. (2017). Effects of Singing Bowl Sound Meditation on Mood, Tension, and Well-being: An

Observational Study. <em>Journal of Evidence-Based Complementary & Alternative Medicine</em>, <em>22</em>(3), 401–406. https://doi.org/10.1177/2156587216668109

Guyer, J. J., Maddux, W. W., Barden, J., & Kim, H. (2021). Falling Vocal Intonation Signals Speaker Confidence and Conditionally Boosts Persuasion. *Journal of Experimental Social Psychology*, *92*, 104085. https://doi.org/10.1016/j.jesp.2020.104085

H., B. (2021, July 15). <i>Hoodoo Folk Magic: How to Use the Horseshoe - The Hoodoo Shop</i>. The Hoodoo Shop. Retrieved from https://thehoodooshop.com/hoodoo-horseshoe/

Hall, R. (2017). *Hex Workers: African American Women, Hoodoo, and Power in the Nineteenth- and Early Twentieth-Century U.S.* (Master's thesis, Cleveland State University). EngagedScholarship@CSU. https://engagedscholarship.csuohio.edu/etd_master/1206/
Kelly, J. L. (2019). Cemetery hoodoo: Culture, ritual crime and forensic archaeology. *Forensic Science International: Synergy*, *1*, 17–28. https://doi.org/10.1016/j.fsisyn.2019.09.002
Simmons, A. M. (2000). The Power of Hoodoo: African Relic Symbolism in Amistad and The Narrative of Frederick Douglass, an American Slave. *The Oswald Review: An International Journal of Undergraduate Research and Criticism in the Discipline of English*, *2*(1). https://scholarcommons.sc.edu/tor/vol2/iss1/5/

Hargrove, J. (2018). Hoodoo, Conjure, and Folk Magic: A Look at Traditional African American Folk Magic. *Journal of Black Studies*, *49*(7), 753-769.

Hazzard-Donald, K. (2013). <i>Conjure Culture: Hoodoo and the Roots of the Blues</i>. University of Illinois Press.

Hazzard-Donald, K. (2013). *Mojo Workin': The Old African American Picture of Good and Evil*. University of Illinois Press. https://doi.org/10.5406/j.ctt2tt7gh

Holloway, J. E. (2005). <i>Africanisms in American Culture</i> (2nd ed.). Indiana University Press.

Institute for Natural Medicine. (2026). <i>Ensuring the Quality, Safety, and Health Benefits of Herbs, Mushrooms, Algae, and Lichen Botanicals</i>. Retrieved from https://www.naturemed.org/post/ensuring-the-quality-safety-and-health-benefits-of-herbs-mushrooms-algae-and-lichen-botanicals

Lemon8. (2025, May 17). *Hoodoo & Herbal Spiritual Baths: My Cleansing Ritual for Protection*. Retrieved from Wikipedia contributors. (2026, April 19). *Hoodoo (spirituality)*. In Wikipedia, The Free Encyclopedia. Retrieved 12:06, April 26, 2026, from

Lina. (2025, October 14). <i>Folklore + Uses of Ritual Black Salt</i>. Heart + Lore. Retrieved from https://heartandlore.com/blogs/articles/the-folklore-uses-of-ritual-black-salt

Llewellyn. (2023). <i>Waning Moon Magic: Banishing, Releasing & Protection Spells</i>. Llewellyn Worldwide. https://www.llewellyn.com/journal/article/2996

Long, C. A. (2023). Mississippi River Valley Voodoo: A Living Tradition? <i>UC Press Journals</i>.

Long, C. F. (2001). <i>Spiritual Merchants: Religion, Magic, and Commerce</i>. University of Tennessee Press.

Long, C. M. (2001). <em>Spiritual merchants: Religion, magic, and commerce</em>. University of Tennessee Press.

LoveHerbsOnTheHill.com. (2025, September 20). <i>Basil Folklore, Magic & Rituals | Herbs on the Hill</i>. Retrieved from https://www.loveherbsonthehill.com/blogs/herbs/basil-folklore-magic-rituals

Ma, X., Yue, Z. Q., Gong, Z. Q., Zhang, H., Duan, N. Y., Shi, Y. T., ... & Li, Y. (2017). The Effect of Diaphragmatic Breathing on Attention, Negative Affect and Stress in Healthy Adults. <i>Frontiers in Psychology</i>, <i>8</i>, 874.

Moerman, D. E. (1998). <i>Native American Ethnobotany</i>. Timber Press.

Murphy, J. M. (1994). <i>Working the Spirit: Ceremonies of the African Diaspora</i>. Beacon Press.

Jar Spells in Hoodoo: Potent Conjurations for Personal Transformation. (2024).

What Is Hoodoo? A Beginner's Guide to African American Folk Magic | aromaG's Botanica. (2025). <em>aromaG's Botanica</em>.

What is Hoodoo? A Guide to the History of Rootwork - Original Botanica. (2025). <em>Original Botanica</em>.

Original Botanica. (2024). *Understanding Sympathetic Magic: Principles and Practices*. Retrieved from https://originalbotanica.com/blogs/news/sympathetic-magic-principles-practices

Original Botanica. (2025, April 14). *What is Hoodoo? A Guide to the History of Rootwork*. https://www.originalbotanica.com/blog/what-is-hoodoo-history-rootwork-guide/

Original Botanica. (2024). *Understanding Sympathetic Magic: Principles and Practices*. Retrieved from https://originalbotanica.com/blogs/news/sympathetic-magic-principles-practices; My Cousins Coven. (2025). *Sympathetic Magic*. Retrieved from https://www.mycousinscoven.com/sympathetic-magic

Original Botanica. (2025). *What is Hoodoo? A Guide to the History of Rootwork*. Original Botanica Blog. Retrieved from https://www.originalbotanica.com/blog/what-is-hoodoo-history-rootwork/
Chesapeake Conjure Society. (n.d.). *What it Means to Gather: Human and Hoodoo*. Retrieved from https://chesapeakeconjure.org/what-it-means-to-gather
TheQueenPo. (2025, October 1). *What is Hoodoo, 5 Principles of Hoodoo, & Tips to Learn More* [Video]. YouTube. Retrieved from https://www.youtube.com/watch?v=F_YlqA2-W2I

Original Botanica. (2025). *What is Hoodoo? A Guide to the History of Rootwork*. Original Botanica Blog. Retrieved from https://www.originalbotanica.com/blog/what-is-hoodoo-history-rootwork/
Lemon8. (2025, June 3). *What is Root Work? Understanding Hoodoo & Modern Rootworkers*. Retrieved from https://www.lemon8-app.com/lemon8/discover?q=What%20is%20Root%20Work?

%20Understanding%20Hoodoo%20&%20Modern%20Rootworkers&from=search

Otherworldly Oracle. (2020, January 14). <i>Waning Moon Magic: Binding, Banishing and Releasing Rituals</i>. Otherworldly Oracle. https://otherworldlyoracle.com/waning-moon-magic/

Penczak, C. (2014, January 13). <i>Planetary Magic 7: Saturn, Karma and Protection</i>. Christopher Penczak. https://christopherpenczak.com/2014/01/13/planetary-magic-7-saturn-karma-and-protection/
Yusuf, A. (2020, April 25). <i>Planetary Days: Saturdays and Saturn</i>. Alicia Yusuf. https://aliciayusuf.com/planetary-days-saturdays-and-saturn/

Petty, R. E., Briñol, P., & Tormala, Z. L. (2009). The effects of body posture on self-evaluation: A new look at the "attitude–behavior" relationship. *European Journal of Social Psychology*, *39*(1), 38–49. https://doi.org/10.1002/ejsp.529

Pratt, M. (2024, September 5). *5 Minutes of Mindfulness Brings Real Benefits, According to Science*. Mindful. https://www.mindful.org/5-minutes-of-mindfulness-brings-real-benefits-according-to-science/

Pratt, M. (2025, May 13). *A science-backed guide to mindful breathing*. National Geographic. https://www.nationalgeographic.com/science/article/mindful-breathing-science-benefits

PushBlack Spirit. (2024, October 2). *The Undeniable Role Salt And Water Play In Our Spirituality*. PushBlack Spirit. Retrieved from Original Botanica. (2023, June 27). *Spiritual & Magical Uses For Salt*. Original Botanica. Retrieved from Homes & Gardens. (2023, March 27). *More than just a seasoning, salt could be the surprisingly spiritual tool your home needs, experts say*. Retrieved from

Seattle Opera. (2024). <i>More than Music: The Hidden Messages in Spirituals</i>. Seattle Opera Blog. https://www.seattleopera.org/community--education/blog/2024/more-than-music/

Sweet, F. S. (2013). <i>Black freedom by the book</i>. Oxford University Press.

T., E. (2021, March 19). <i>Hoodoo Baths: Cleansing and Spiritual Baths in

Hoodoo - The Hoodoo Shop</i>. The Hoodoo Shop. Retrieved from https://thehoodooshop.com/hoodoo-baths/

The Conjure Shop. (2023, May 22). <i>Lodestone in Hoodoo: What It Is, How It Works, and How to Use It</i>. Retrieved from https://theconjureshop.com/blogs/articles/lodestone-in-hoodoo

The Conjure Shop. (2023, April 20). <i>Railroad Spikes in Hoodoo: Protection, Binding, and Drawing Power</i>. Retrieved from https://theconjureshop.com/blogs/articles/railroad-spikes-in-hoodoo

The Life Potion. (2025, January 5). *The Origin of Florida Water and how it is made and used*. The Life Potion. Retrieved from Rock Collage. (2024, November 14). *21 Spiritual and Ritual Uses of Florida Water*. Rock Collage. Retrieved from The Divine Feminine. (2021, October 20). *Origins and Spiritual Uses of Florida Water*. The Divine Feminine. Retrieved from

The Outdoor Apothecary. (2021). <i>9 Basic Principles Of Ethical Wildcrafting For Beginners - The Outdoor Apothecary</i>. Retrieved from https://www.theoutdoorapothecary.com/ethical-wildcrafting/

Tian, L., Yu, J., & Mao, H. (2017). The usefulness of the useless: How ritualized behavior improves self-control under competition pressure. <em>Journal of Sport and Health Science</em>, <em>6</em>(4), 512–518.

Ting, S. C. (2011). The Literary Heritage of African-American Trickster Tales. <i>The Journal of American Folklore</i>, <i>124</i>(492), 37–64.

Tyrant Farms. (2022). <i>Solomon's seal (& false Solomon's seal) - how to grow, forage & eat - Tyrant Farms</i>. Retrieved from https://www.tyrantfarms.com/solomons-seal/

Tyson, D. (2018). <i>Practical Solomonic Magic</i>. Llewellyn Worldwide.

Uhl, C. (2019, October 07). <i>Magic of the Crossroads - Flying the Hedge</i>. Retrieved from https://flyingthehedge.com/magic-of-the-crossroads/

High John the Conqueror Root is a legendary botanical talisman in Hoodoo, known for conferring strength, courage, mastery over challenges, and triumph over adversity, rooted in African American folklore and practices of resilience

(Curio, Craft & Conjure, n.d.; Magic Fairy Candles, n.d.; The Power of High John the Conqueror Root in Hoodoo, 2025; EBSCO, n.d.; Art Of The Root, 2024; Ginseng, Hoodoo, and the Magic of Upholding African American Earth-Based Traditions, 2021).

Virginia & Rook. (2024, March 26). *The Origins of Hoodoo: Spirituality and Cultural Significance*. Virginia & Rook. https://virginiaandrook.com/blogs/news/the-origins-of-hoodoo-spirituality-and-cultural-significance

Wellspring Center for Prevention. (2024, July 23). *The Benefits of Positive Affirmations*. https://www.wellspringprevention.org/blog/the-benefits-of-positive-affirmations/

Whitehouse, H., & McKay, R. (Eds.). (2014). <em>Ritual, Emotion, and Memory: Explorations in Social, Cultural, and Cognitive Anthropology</em>. Oxford University Press.

Wikipedia. (n.d.). *Hoodoo (spirituality)*. Retrieved April 25, 2026, from https://en.wikipedia.org/wiki/Hoodoo_(spirituality)

Yronwode, C. (2001). <i>Hoodoo Herb and Root Magic</i>. Lucky Mojo Curio Co.

Yronwode, C. (2002). <i>Candle Color Correspondences in Hoodoo, Conjure, and Rootwork</i>. Lucky Mojo Curio Co. https://www.luckymojo.com/candlemagiccolors.html

Yronwode, C. (2002). <i>High John the Conqueror Root</i>. Lucky Mojo Curio Co. https://www.luckymojo.com/highjohn.html

Yronwode, C. (2002). <em>Hoodoo Herb and Root Magic</em>. Lucky Mojo Curio Co. https://www.luckymojo.com/hoodooherbs.html

Yronwode, C. (2002). <i>Hoodoo Herb and Root Magic: A Materia Magica of African-American Conjure</i>. Lucky Mojo Curio Co.

Yronwode, C. (2002). <em>Hoodoo Herb and Rootwork</em>. Lucky Mojo Curio Co.

Yronwode, C. (2019). <i>Hoodoo Herb and Root Magic: A Materia Magica of

African-American Conjure</i>. Lucky Mojo Curio Co.

Yronwode, C. (n.d.). <em>Hoodoo Attraction Spells</em>. Lucky Mojo Curio Co. https://www.luckymojo.com/attraction.html

Yronwode, C. (n.d.). <em>The Rootwork and Hoodoo Spells of Papa Jim</em>. Lucky Mojo Curio Co. https://www.luckymojo.com/papajim.html

aromaG's Botanica. (2025, April 23). *What Is Hoodoo? A Beginner's Guide to African American Folk Magic*. https://www.aromagsbotanica.com/what-is-hoodoo-a-beginners-guide/

aromaG's Botanica. (2025, August 13). *How to Use Red Brick Dust for Protection*. Retrieved from Cajun Conjuror. (n.d.). *Home Protection Renewal*. Retrieved from

aromaG's Botanica. (2025, August 13). *How to Use Red Brick Dust for Protection*. Retrieved from Wax Spiritual. (n.d.). *Red Brick Dust*. Retrieved from Cajun Conjuror. (n.d.). *Home Protection Renewal*. Retrieved from

www.ingramcontent.com/pod-product-compliance
Lightning Source LLC
LaVergne TN
LVHW010914110826
845149LV00013B/2359